How to Get That Job

HOW TO GET THAT JOB

by FRED D. NEWELL

with a foreword by Frank S. Endicott

NORTHLAND PRESS / FLAGSTAFF

To my family who stood by patiently
while this book was written.

Contents

Contents

Contents

Foreword

MOST PEOPLE, whether they are willing to admit it or not, need help in finding the best possible job. It may not be difficult to get employment of some kind, but it is not likely to be easy to get the particular job that offers the most opportunity, reward and satisfaction. It is the purpose of this book to offer the help which many job-seekers need.

A glance at the table of contents will show that the book is complete. It deals with almost all of the many problems relating to employment. In addition to general information which is helpful, there are specific suggestions regarding how to use the services of a placement office, how to apply for a job, how to be prepared for the employment interview, how to develop a good resume and much more. It is a practical book.

The book is also personal. It is aimed directly at you, the reader. It is a reflection of the personal philosophy and values of the author and there is a good deal of straight-forward advice based upon his many years of experience in military service, business and education.

Someone has said that there are two kinds of people in the world, those who write books and those who read them. There is also a third kind — those who *use* books. This book is intended

Foreword

to be used. It is a guide which can be followed in making one of life's most important decisions, namely, the choice of a job. For many, especially the young college graduate, this turns out to be the choice of a career.

Frank S. Endicott

Professor of Education, Emeritus
Director of Placement, Retired
Northwestern University

Preface

FOR THIRTY-FIVE YEARS, serving as a teacher, a physical training instructor, a businessman, and an administrator, I have observed the difficulties that many have in securing employment, and the recurrence of the same problems: preparation of a resume, writing letters of inquiry and application, knowing the ethics involved in securing employment.

My initial recognition of this challenge came upon graduation from college. There I stood with the diploma in one hand but without the slightest notion of how to secure employment. Through trial and error I learned by doing. I had not been taught the rudimentary skills needed for job hunting. College officials assisted with all the knowledge they had at that time.

In 1966 and 1967 at the University of Northern Colorado as I was doing advanced graduate study, major emphasis was placed on College Student Personnel Work. My interest in job placement was rekindled since applicants for employment in the 1970s were having the same problems encountered by students of the 1930s.

I sought out educators, placement officials, employers, and students and found that in many instances students were still not being taught how to prepare themselves adequately for job hunting. In a critique of my original manuscript one graduate student commented: "I will bet that sixty-five percent of the students graduating from college today have not been taught the things contained in your book."

xiii

Preface

Job hunting can be one of the most important, difficult, and challenging assignments an individual ever undertakes. Hope makes it easier. Hope is enhanced by confidence, desire, dedication, and determination. Believing in yourself is the catalyst.

I would hope that this book has something for every job hunter regardless of status or age to serve as a guide in job-seeking.

These data were checked for accuracy at the time of publication; it is possible that by the time this book is read, changes may have occurred. Addresses may change, companies may go out of business, and policies of firms may be revised.

Exploring the problems of job seeking has generated many creative approaches. Resolution of these approaches will require the effort and thought of many from within and without educational institutions and the world of business. New demands will continue to be placed on education, governmental agencies, and industry to aid the job seeker to find suitable employment.

During the seven years of research, some one hundred and fifty Directors of Placement in junior colleges, colleges, universities, business colleges and technical schools were reached, either in person or by letter, in addition to the Library of Congress, governmental agencies at the federal, state, and local levels. Especially helpful were Dr. Kenneth Hogan, Professor of Education and former Director of Placement, University of Northern Colorado; Mr. Stanton Peckham, Book Editor, *The Denver Post;* Mr. Wylie Smith, Public Information Office, Northern Arizona University; Mrs. Marion Lyday, Editorial Consultant, and Dr. James Otto Berg, Assistant Dean, College of Education, Northern Arizona University. Others whose help assisted me greatly were the many colleagues who read the manuscript, the reference staffs of the libraries of the University of Northern Colorado and Northern Arizona University. To the many students and faculty and staff members who inspired and encouraged me, my grateful thanks.

FRED D. NEWELL

1

Basic Information for All Job Seekers

No man can go far who never sets his foot down until he knows the sidewalk is under it. No man has earned the right to intellectual ambition until he has learned to lay his course by a star he has never seen — to dig by divining rods for springs which he will never reach.

Justice Oliver Wendell Holmes

START LOOKING NOW

NOW THAT ACADEMIC WORK for the chosen profession — teaching, business, industry or perhaps a position with a government agency — at the local, state or national level — has almost been completed, it is time to think about a career and getting a job. According to the 1970 College Placement Annual — "There is a lot of difference between starting a career . . . a job is a way of earning a living, but 'a career is a way of living' . . . it is the way you want to live."

Now is the time to start preparing those all-important credentials, references and resumes. You must do an effective job of selling yourself on these pieces of paper because they are screened before the interview by prospective employers. These items are all important to you and the better you are prepared, the better the chances are of landing a job.

This book is designed to help you to be totally prepared when that job opportunity comes along.

Start Looking Now

The resume, sometimes called a vita, describes personal goals and qualifications while the references are what others think of and how they rate an individual. Prepare this carefully because it represents what you have done to equip yourself for life.

Seeking a job will be a totally new educational experience because this is something very few have done, especially the young graduate who enters a job market in which he may work the rest of his life.

Hopefully, you have started to prepare yourself for this crucial situation long before you have obtained that degree. Good grades as well as leadership qualities and extra-curricular participation always look good to the prospective employer.

A pleasing personality as well as a neat, attractive appearance will also be among the many things weighed and evaluated by those doing the interviewing. Experience is important sometimes; however, an interesting background and an eagerness to learn will often mean as much as experience.

In looking over the initial job-seeking situation, you may find yourself confronted with many confusing and complicated questions, such as: What kind of letter should I write inquiring about a vacancy? How should I go about writing for additional information? How should I go about writing a letter when applying for a position?

Other frequent questions include: How should I conduct myself during an interview? What should I say? What should I wear? Should I sit quietly and let the interviewer proceed with the questioning? What salary should I ask?

If you are "totally prepared" you will know something about all of these areas before the interview takes place and you can give intelligent answers as well as ask intelligent questions.

Each interviewer has his job to do — that of hiring the best possible person available. If you are not prepared, others will be. By presenting your true energetic self, chances are good that you can land that job!

The career placement service, from the college or university from which you have been graduated, should have these credentials (resume, recommendations and other critical papers) on file. These placement specialists can help answer your questions in the preparation of these credentials. They are interested in helping you find a job. Private placement agencies can render a similar service.

Learning something about the position you are seeking as well as something about the school district with which you are seeking an interview, something about the firm or agency, will make the interview go more smoothly. If a specific geographic location is desired, knowledge about this area is also impressive.

According to Paul W. Boynton, author of *Six Ways to Get a Job*, the six ways to find a job are:

1. College and University Placement Bureaus
2. State and Commercial Employment Agencies
3. Personal Solicitation
4. Letters of Application
5. Commercial Advertising in Newspapers and Magazines
6. Information from Friends and Relatives

These six methods, of course, vary in their degree of effectiveness, depending on your age, experience, goals, ambition, and personal circumstances.

However, surveys indicate the college placement service is by far the most popular recruitment source used by those employing college-trained personnel. This is substantiated by the March 15, 1971, issue of the *U. S. News & World Report* which states, "Hunt for employment will take graduating seniors down a long road. First stop is the college placement office, where job offers are listed, interviews arranged." These agencies help prepare credentials as well as keep students informed of campus visits by recruiters. It is essential to point out that the final responsibility for finding a job rests with you, and, therefore, every avenue which may lead to "the right job" should be explored.

3

Placement Registration

The better you are prepared, the quicker you can start seeking employment and the better chance you will have to secure a position.

Placement services across the nation vary in their approach. Become familiar with your placement service.

In order for the placement service to be of assistance, you should make an appointment for an interview with a member of the placement staff. It is important for you to complete applications, completely and neatly. A prospective employer is interested in brief, exact details.

Faith in yourself to adapt quickly while projecting a true image is of prime importance. Believe in yourself! At times, these procedures seem useless, but they all have an important purpose. For each student a placement service places, the better it looks, so no one is working against you, unless it is yourself!

PLACEMENT REGISTRATION

To make the job easier, this information has been compiled to assist you in your job-seeking adventure.

Normally college placement services hold fall meetings for seniors who will be graduating in the spring or summer. Many hold meetings at other times of the year to assist other students. During these meetings, complete instructions, along with placement materials, are given to prospective graduates. These materials must be completed and returned as soon as possible. Private and/or State Department of Employment agencies operate independently under their own governing rules.

You can find a good job; however, not too many good jobs will find you.

WHY REGISTER WITH THE CAREER PLACEMENT SERVICE?

Most employing officials will consult a placement service official for information concerning candidates who are college graduates.

An interviewing official will ordinarily look credentials over carefully before the interview; so they must be in proper order.

In seeking a position on your own initiative, it is frequently advantageous to inform employing officials that credentials are on file in the placement service of the school from which you have, or will, graduate. If other placement services also have credentials, list title, location and address of these offices. Hopefully, one complete set of credentials will or should be located at the same place. You should make sure your credentials are up-to-date.

Many opportunities for employment are lost because of the lapse of time necessary to get resumes and references together to make up credentials you have not previously registered with the placement service. After all, employers are interested in people who are interested in themselves.

The placement service is in a position to learn about vacancies. If you are registered with the placement service you will be notified about all positions for which you are qualified.

Placement services permit the keeping of permanent files of letters and recommendations that are often irreplaceable.

WHO MAY REGISTER?

If you are a college student who plans on completing the required number of hours at the institution from which you plan to graduate, you are eligible for placement service help. Many jobs require degrees; if you are not graduating you will need to check your placement service to see if you are entitled to assistance. Some placement services have reciprocal agreements with placement services in other colleges, and assist each other's graduates. Many placement services require a remarkably low number of hours earned at their institutions before rendering assistance. What are the requirements at your school?

At many institutions of higher learning, registering with the placement service is a requirement for graduation if you are a candidate for a degree. This insures that the placement service will be

5

able to help in securing a job, although you are in no way obligated to use this assistance.

Placement services maintain active and inactive files on students. The active registrants include all current graduates as well as many alumni who request having their credentials remain in the active file. Most of these alumni want their files to be in an active status in case they change jobs. Active status varies from institution to institution; however, generally a person is active from approximately one to five years or until he finds a job. The inactive person is one not seeking employment; however, he may request that his file be placed in active status at any time after he has brought his credentials up-to-date. This can be accomplished by submitting requested material about himself. This will help assure his getting the job for which he is applying.

Some placement services have a small charge for their service. Others will be free. If there is a charge, this is money well spent, because a commercial placement agency will charge considerably more for the same service. Before signing a contract with a commercial firm to help you find a job, know exactly what its charge will be and the service you will get for this fee. Generally this will be a percentage of your first few checks; so this will be a bill that will have to be paid promptly or it could place your newly found job in jeopardy for being delinquent in paying your bill.

WHAT YOU CAN EXPECT
FROM THE CAREER PLACEMENT SERVICE

The placement service will use every effort, as far as your qualifications permit, to help in securing employment. The office, with the assistance of the heads of departments, deans and professors, makes recommendations in line with requirements for the position actively being sought.

The degree of service the placement service is able to give depends on several factors, such as vacancies listed, your relative standing with others seeking the same position, experience in the field, age, or some special ability specified by the employer.

Modesty gets one nowhere fast. If you have made a significant contribution in some area or have been given a special award, make sure this is included in the placement file. It may seem small and trivial; however, this may be the thing that helps land that job!

Being pleasantly persistent, while not being overly aggressive, will let a prospective employer know you are vitally interested in the job he has to offer. However, do not be pushy and demanding.

Personality plays a big part in job placement. The number of graduates being employed during any given year will depend mainly on how efficiently the placement service has served employing officials in the past, how well alumni are giving satisfaction on their present jobs, and how earnestly each applicant seeks a position.

Each set of credentials will be kept on file by the placement service and you may refer to the placement service when applying for a position. By providing evidence that a vacancy exists, the placement service will forward credentials to any place requested by you.

Some college and university placement services will not help fill a vacancy that has been turned over to a commercial placement agency, and some will. Know the local policy.

It is necessary for the employing official to express interest in you before credentials are sent to him. The placement service will send credentials to other institutions' placement services, once you have requested this. At least one complete file should be on record at a place of your choosing.

OBLIGATIONS OF EACH REGISTRANT

Promptly fill out all forms accurately and neatly, preferably with a typewriter, when first registering with the placement service. Be sure that the keys are clean and free from being plugged up with ink. If handwritten, blue or black ink may be used; however, print or write legibly.

These are *your* records; make sure they are kept up-to-date. It is very important that you notify the service about changes of address, changes of position, changes of marital status, additional schooling and experience, personal accomplishments and/or any other relevant information.

You can help by notifying the placement service of vacancies you are not interested in or not qualified for. If notified of a vacancy, it is extremely necessary to report to the placement service even though the position is not desirable. This helps the placement service find someone else. This procedure helps employers keep an interest in the placement service, knowing it is doing everything possible to fill the position.

When you receive a notice of a vacancy from the placement service, if it interests you, make application by letter, telegram or telephone to the employer named, unless it is asked that these methods not be used. Perhaps this employer will be making a visit to your campus. After initial contact, if no answer is received within a week or ten days, a follow-up letter should be sent.

Consult with a member of the placement service staff if additional information is needed in taking further steps to contact a prospective employer. The help from personnel in the placement service cannot be overemphasized.

All notices from placement services are confidential. This information should not be discussed with other candidates or persons who may not respect the confidential nature of this information. These policies are set up for your protection. You frequently will bring yourself into competition from others by broadcasting information on vacancies and frequently someone with sub-par standards will apply, which could hurt your employment chances. The placement service has a responsibility to the employing officials to help control the applications to be reviewed. Obviously, a prospective employer cannot talk with every student. He is seeking a qualified person and unless the placement service helps him find one, this employer may start seeking the help of other placement services.

Once a position has been accepted, the placement service should be notified at your earliest opportunity. Failure to do this will hinder the placement service in helping other students to be placed. At the end of the school year, the placement service must know the status of every candidate if it is to do an effective job. Even if the placement service has not helped in finding a position, it should know that a job has been found. *Cooperation from both sides is essential.*

PERSONAL ADJUSTMENT TO THE WORLD OF WORK

If past graduates from your school have performed well, prospective employers will come looking for more good students; however, if they have not performed well, you will have to do a superb job of presenting yourself. This is why frank opinions should be given on letters of recommendation.

Regardless of the field, you need source information when applying for a job, especially when applying for the first time. A "regular" job should be approached with a different attitude than is used when applying for a "part-time" job while in school.

When studying the resource material, you should become familiar with these objectives:

1. Become acquainted with the employer's philosophy.
2. Seek help in developing a plan for achieving career goals.
3. Assist in selecting, obtaining and keeping a position commensurate with individual goals and interests.
4. Review and analyze the benefits inherent in the democratic form of government and the American system of "Free Enterprise."
5. Focus on responsibilities as a member of a business or professional group, the community and society in general.
6. Know what you expect and what is expected of you.

9

Besides studying information contained within this book, the above information will help you go into the interview with the attitude that "I am the one for the job," and knowing that you are "totally prepared."

Announcements of job openings, throughout the school year, will be made to you by mail, telephone, and bulletin boards; however, if you are eager to get a job you will check with the office on your own. Perhaps a job vacancy has just arrived.

Many placement services keep cumulative alphabetical card files of all job openings which have been called to the attention of the placement office. These records are good sources of information on the types of jobs currently available to college graduates.

The bulletin board is the prime medium used to notify students that specific companies, firms or school district personnel will be on campus to conduct interviews. Generally these announcements will be at the office, but many individual colleges, schools and departments will also have them.

By checking these bulletin boards on a regular basis, you will have maximum opportunity for an interview with a desirable employer. General notices may be posted for several weeks while specific and last-minute notices may appear only a few days before the interviewer is on campus.

A campus visitation schedule, pertaining to representatives coming to the campus, posted on the bulletin board will give the name of the company, date of visit, types of positions open, qualifications required, and other pertinent information.

Underclassmen interested in a specific company, firm or school district will find this a good opportunity to start becoming prepared before they face the interview in a year or two.

Specific jobs for individuals having special qualifications might be listed separately or with specific colleges, schools or departments. It is best for you to be on your toes and keep a constant check on all possibilities.

Periodically the placement service may take announcements of a general nature that should be called to everyone's attention. Generally mass meetings are held to cover these items.

If open during vacations, holidays or breaks between semesters or quarters, the placement service may contact you about job openings by telephone or mail. Make sure the placement service has your current address and telephone number.

Whenever possible, special notices will be published in the school newspaper or aired over campus radio and television stations.

OBTAINING AN INTERVIEW

Prior to requesting an interview, you should study pamphlets and brochures on various job possibilities. Some of this literature can be located in the placement service office. Other directories related to jobs can be found in well-stocked libraries.

While studying this literature, you may find your first area of interest is not the type of work you would like. By doing as much preliminary checking and planning as possible, you can better choose your job. By choosing the right job early in your career, you can advance more rapidly by doing a good job because you are satisfied with what you are doing.

Approximately four to six weeks before an interviewing representative will arrive on campus, the placement service will make this visit known to all who are interested.

Make appointments through the placement secretary as early as possible because interview time is occasionally limited, especially if the representative will be on campus for a short period of time. If all of the interview time is taken, then leave your name and telephone number, in case of cancellations. Most interviewers will extend themselves to see you if they think you are genuinely interested in a job.

Sometimes jobs are filled quicker than anticipated and recruitment trips may be cancelled. Also, an additional recruiter may be sent and if the placement service is expecting this, additional space

11

can be provided. This also permits extra scheduling of people interested in a particular job.

Campus interviews are usually conducted in one of the private interviewing rooms within the placement service. Show up early for the interview and double check the room number and time of the interview with the placement secretary. By being early, perhaps more time will be allowed for your interview. If at all possible, if an appointment for an interview cannot be kept, notify the secretary as soon as possible. This may permit someone else to use your cancelled interview time.

How reliable is a person who makes appointments and does not keep them time after time? The placement service has a responsibility to all seeking jobs, not just one.

Interviews at the employer's office or some other designated place are held from time to time, especially if an interviewer cannot be sent to the campus. This may require that you travel to some distant point, ordinarily at your own expense. These interviews can be arranged between you and the employer, or through joint efforts with placement service officials. If you are to be interviewed at the employer's place of business, then the placement service should be notified far enough in advance so that credentials can be mailed to reach the proper destination prior to the interview. Even though an appointment has been made, if employment has already been accepted elsewhere, notify all parties concerned immediately regarding the cancellation of your interview; this school district or company may be a future employer.

PRE-INTERVIEW PLANNING

Prior to the interview it is important for you to know something about the organization, the community, the interviewer, and the various resources of its particular section of the country.

It is advisable to know something about the likes and dislikes of the person doing the interviewing. For example, if you know the interviewer is a stamp collector, you might ask him about the extent of his collection. Do not make this too obvious nor belabor the subject excessively. An appropriate move of this nature oftentimes can help to bring about a relaxed atmosphere. Too, mutual agreement on almost any subject can often benefit both parties involved.

If a school district or company's name has an unusual pronunciation, learn how to pronounce it correctly. If you can discuss briefly some facts pertaining to the school or company this often will enhance your employment chances.

If you get advance knowledge prior to or during the interview, that a large turnover in personnel occurred in the past in the position you are being interviewed for, you may want to know why. *You will want to know what happened to the person/persons who were formerly in that position and how long each of them stayed.* Did he/they resign? Were they promoted? Were they fired? If so, why? The answers could affect your decision to accept the job, if offered. By being prepared, equipped and flexible, you can more easily talk from a position of strength.

Sometimes organizations will have had both successes and failures. Be aware of them and be able to discuss them from an understanding point of view. If you have a solution to their problem, be certain of your position and state how you would go about remedying their situation, if hired.

If information is not available in pamphlets and brochures regarding the geographic location of the area you are interested in, check a road atlas, an encyclopedia, the World Almanac, the yellow pages of an appropriate telephone directory, and write to the Chamber of Commerce of the town you are interested in. Any of these sources will provide you with information. Another source of information is the newspaper in the locality in which you are interested. You can either subscribe to one, or you can find one in a library or newsstand.

These publications often list many key things such as local

schools, hospitals, churches, recreational facilities, and will give you an indication about working in a particular community.

CHECK LIST TO USE BEFORE INTERVIEWS

Many people find it is necessary to review for an examination. For the same reason, it is suggested that you review for an interview. Almost all of the items listed below have been called to the attention of the placement services by school or company representatives across the nation that interview applicants. Below is a guide for you to follow in preparing for an interview.

I. INFORMATION ABOUT THE SCHOOL OR COMPANY
  A. Know the company background, its business, products, and other relevant information.
  B. Know why you are interested in the company.
  C. Know the location of the company.
  D. Have at least two good questions prepared to ask about the company, its products, its policies, and its long-range goals.

II. PREPARING FOR THE INTERVIEW
  A. Take a personal inventory of yourself and know your goals.
  B. Be able to tell in two minutes the potential you can offer the company.
  C. Bring a filled pen, a pencil, and notepaper.
  D. Learn the interviewer's name and title.
  E. Read all directions on literature given you and fill out application blanks accurately.
  F. Know definitions and terminology in your field.
  G. Be at least five minutes early.

BEING HONEST WITH YOURSELF

Do not wait until the night before the interview to start preparing yourself for an interview. You should start on this weeks ahead of time. After you rate yourself on the SELF-ANALYSIS CHECK LIST and find yourself lacking in one or more areas, then avail yourself of the opportunity to use the assistance of one of the counseling services listed below. The people giving these services can be a great asset to you. Do not be afraid to seek assistance from these people. If you have a problem you have to admit it before you can really be helped.

Being capable of looking in the mirror and being honest with yourself and making a straightforward analysis of what you see are important aspects. Being honest is being able to recognize a weak spot within yourself and is being able and not afraid to do something about it.

The SELF-ANALYSIS CHECK LIST is included to give you an opportunity to make a self-appraisal of your personal attributes. The main purpose is to stimulate your thinking. It is as important to know your good qualities as it is to be able to recognize your liabilities so that you can correct them. How can you correct something if you do not know it exists?

Be honest when filling out the rating sheet. If you think you rate "good," then check it; however, if you think you rate "average" or "poor," mark these accordingly.

The following self-appraisal check list is by no means an all-inclusive list that will foretell the future; it is merely another way to help you prepare for the interview.

SELF-ANALYSIS CHECK LIST

Personality Traits	*Good*	*Average*	*Poor*
1. Ability to get along with others	____	____	____
2. Dependability and reliability	____	____	____
3. Initiative	____	____	____
4. Capacity for hard work	____	____	____
5. Resourcefulness	____	____	____
6. Enthusiasm	____	____	____

Self-Analysis Check List

Personality Traits	*Good*	*Average*	*Poor*
7. Facility at expression, both orally and in writing	___	___	___
8. Ability to take constructive criticism	___	___	___
9. Cooperativeness	___	___	___
10. Self-confidence	___	___	___
11. Honesty	___	___	___
12. Integrity	___	___	___
13. Regard for the rights of others	___	___	___
14. Personal appearance	___	___	___
15. Bearing	___	___	___
16. Personality	___	___	___
17. Courtesy	___	___	___
18. Cheerfulness	___	___	___
19. Friendliness	___	___	___
20. Freedom from fear	___	___	___
21. Professional courtesy	___	___	___
22. Humaneness	___	___	___
23. Promptness and efficiency	___	___	___
24. Faithfulness	___	___	___
25. Loyalty	___	___	___

Examine each trait where you scored less than "good" with the thought of finding methods to improve yourself regarding that particular characteristic. You should prepare a written plan to follow in improving the qualities where you scored "average" or "poor" and follow your plan. Remember that admitting a weakness is the first step to eliminating it!

The following services are possible sources where you can get additional assistance to determine ways to improve the poorer qualities on the check list. Having someone to talk to is helpful and it should be someone capable of helping clear up these undesirable traits.

1. Student Counseling Service
2. Professors and/or advisors
3. Clergyman or spiritual guide
4. A physician or psychologist
5. An advisor from the placement service

DRESSING FOR THE INTERVIEW

In the hustle and bustle of getting prepared for the interview it is often likely that important items will be overlooked. A pleasing personal appearance and good personal hygiene will help to start the interview off right. You should dress in conservative good taste, remembering that your grooming expresses your past training and your attitude toward yourself. Keep in mind that you want to make a favorable impression on the interviewer. Here are some tips that can prove to be a valuable asset to you when dressing for the interview. *Remember, first impressions are often lasting.*

MEN

1. Bathe, brush hair and teeth.

2. Have hair trimmed to go with current styles, and/or to satisfy employers that do the hiring.

3. Shave before interview, even if you have to do it at noon.

4. Wear a conservative, freshly pressed suit or clothing appropriate for your field.

5. Wear a clean shirt and a necktie that goes with other companion colors well.

6. Wear plain socks that are a companion color to other clothing accessories. Do not wear white socks with a dark suit.

WOMEN

1. Bathe, brush hair and teeth.

2. Have a neat hairdo. If hair is bleached make sure the roots do not show and if a wig is used, style it.

3. Wear conservative lipstick and nail polish.

4. Dress conservatively, wear a simple suit or dress that has been freshly laundered.

5. Be moderate with use of perfume.

6. Make sure nylons are straight and are of the right size. Flesh-tone color is satisfactory in most instances.

Men	Women
7. Have shoes shined and avoid runover heels.	7. Wear conservative shoes and avoid flat, backless, or strapless shoes. Wearing a medium or high heel shoe will enhance one's carriage.
8. Have fingernails trim and clean.	
9. Do not wear gaudy items such as unusual rings and chains.	8. Have fingernails well manicured.
	9. Be conservative with use of jewelry. Large and flashy items are often distracting.

People often say "little things mean a lot" and these little things are occasionally overlooked. Prepare your apparel the night before and avoid last-minute frustrating rushes because this makes it hard to relax.

Here are some additional things to be aware of. It is too obvious if you purchase a new pair of shoes and wear them to the interview. They should have been worn several times over a period of two or three months and be well-shined. By the same token, you should not have holes in the soles of your shoes. This could cause the interviewer to think, for some reason, that you are overly desperate for a job, which could lead him to think things that are not true. If you are desperate you ordinarily do not think clearly.

Another point to be considered is to have a clean, unused handkerchief handy. If you have to use it, you can unfold a clean one, not a soiled one.

Men should have their socks pulled up as far as they will go.

You should be well-groomed from the tip of your toes to the top of your head. Remember, you are trying to sell the whole person. Your manner of dress, your intellect, and your bearing reflect you. Be relaxed, yet demonstrate good poise and posture. You should conduct and groom yourself in a manner suitable to the mores of the employer.

A POSITIVE APPROACH

When inquiring about or making application for a job *always use a positive approach.*

Since first impressions are often lasting, it is important that your approach and manner of dress be determined and followed by conventional methods. Employers are interested in individuals who have a positive attitude toward the future; someone who can project a positive quality, image or characteristic; or someone who is proceeding in a direction assumed as beneficial or progressive.

You should use an unequivocal, clear and precise approach to the problem, which is illustrated by the positive versus the negative approach.

THE POSITIVE APPROACH	THE NEGATIVE APPROACH
1. May I inquire as to whether or not you have a vacancy?	1. You don't happen to need some help, do you? What do you pay?
2. If a vacancy does exist, may I have the opportunity of making application for a position with your firm?	2. I won't need to make an application, will I?
3. Upon making application, when do you prefer that I appear for a formal interview?	3. You won't want me to appear for an interview, will you?
4. When will it be most convenient for you to see me?	4. You won't want to see me . . . , will you?
5. I am at your disposal for an interview.	5. I am in a hurry . . . , unless . . . !
6. Someone who is vibrant, radiant, alive and actively seeking employment.	6. One who is decadent, indifferent, lackluster, who is unmoved by the lack of a job prospect and/or possibly happy when a job is not forthcoming.

The applicant should follow the tried, proven and positive approach when seeking a job and avoid the unsure, the negative and doubtful approach.

ETHICS TO BE OBSERVED

Do not apply for a position that is not vacant. Do not pursue an employer when there is no job available, for this may antagonize him.

Qualifications should never be misrepresented; however, good qualities should be stressed in your credentials in a non-bragging manner. Pretending to be trained for a job that you are not qualified for will not work out — it would be tragic for all concerned if you were hired under these conditions.

Underbidding others for a job is not good because if you accept a lesser salary now, an employer might think you are not interested in a raise later on.

It is not ethical to break a contract without obtaining permission from your employer first. Further, it is also not ethical to quit your job without giving your employer proper notice. Ordinarily two weeks notice is required; however, you should know and follow local policy. Normally this should be done in writing. The placement service discourages breaking of contracts at any time. When you are starting to work in a new position you should be particularly careful about this. Your relationship with the placement service can be adversely affected if you should agree to accept a position and before starting to work, you should resign to accept another job. If you do not follow professional ethics it could jeopardize your future in your particular field of work.

Never accept a verbal agreement for employment and hold the employer on a string while seeking another job. What would you think if an employer told you the job was yours and then continued to look for someone else?

In applying for a position all contact should be made with the person responsible for doing the employing, unless you are directed to do otherwise by the employing official.

A position should not be accepted if the requirements and conditions cannot be met. If the employer feels your past experience will help you in adapting to a new area, this is a different situation. If this type of employment is accepted, learn as much about expectations as soon as possible. Do not wait until arriving on the job — get a headstart and by showing this type of initiative, more tolerance will be shown by the employer.

Sometimes employment is given with the provision that summer school will be used by the applicant to get a diploma. If one cannot graduate, the employer should be notified as soon as possible. However, accepting a job, then reneging, is a tactic that shows a lack of decisiveness on the part of the applicant. Securing a new job should be so stimulating and inspirational that better work is actually done by you. However, sickness and family matters can intervene to prevent you from graduating on schedule.

BREACH OF ETHICAL CONDUCT

If you are involved in a breach of ethical conduct, you should be reported directly to the placement officer concerned. The placement service officials should determine if sanctions are to be placed against you. If sanctions should be placed against you they could consist of a warning, a reprimand, a temporary suspension of privileges offered by the placement service and/or a denial of future membership in the sponsoring organization.

INSIDE INTERVIEW TECHNIQUES

When being interviewed, do not *ever* underestimate the person doing the interviewing. There have been instances and records of other than "normal" interviews, when the interviewer asked certain questions just to see what type of reaction he would get out of an applicant.

The questions may differ from time to time. Most frequently, the interviewer is looking for ingenuity, initiative, a quick response, and is testing you to see how you would react under adverse or unusual circumstances. Be prepared to give a "cute," or "clever" answer, but never be sarcastic. Be a creative thinker.

21

Listen Intently

It has been said that Thomas Edison would invite a prospective employee to his home for an evening meal. Soup was always the first course served and if the job seeker salted the soup before tasting it — he did not get the job. Show you have the capacity to think before acting automatically.

Several years ago when women's hosiery had seams, one personnel manager would not make a decision regarding hiring a woman until after she got up and walked out of his office. If her seams were crooked, she did not get the job.

Always be alert, on guard, and remain relaxed. Follow proper social customs, patterns and procedures during an interview. You never know when you may encounter an eccentric interviewer.

By being thoroughly prepared for the interview, being on time, knowing something about the firm, presenting a neat appearance, being knowledgeable in several areas and being gracious to the interviewer *you are presenting your best image. Do not spend four years preparing yourself for employment, then throw them away at the interview table!*

LISTEN INTENTLY

One of the greatest failures in the world is the lack of communication. This not only occurs between people, it occurs between nations. For example, how well do you listen? Do you always interpret things as they sound or do you look for a deeper meaning? Sometimes people are deceptive in trying to catch you off guard. Other times they are serious about trying to slip something by you.

There was an occasion where two people were vying with each other in a contest of wits, which led to the following:

First person: "I will bet you there is a country in South America that has some huge ants, in fact they are so large that many of them weigh a pound."

The second person, being dubious, said: "Let me take your side of the story and I will make you a bet." Imaginary nominal bets were placed.

Second person: "Alright, there is a country in South America that has some huge ants, in fact they are so large that they weigh a pound."

First person: "You lost — pay me your money."

Second person: "No, because I said the same thing you did."

The gist of the whole conversation was that the first person said "many" ants weigh a pound. The second person said there are ants that do weigh a pound. There is a difference between "many" and "one."

Be alert! If you do not understand something, get everything clarified before proceeding with something that cannot be undone after it has been completed. Above all, listen carefully!

TESTS

Some employers will ask that their types of examinations be taken by the applicant, either on campus or later at their establishment. These tests will generally be objective in nature which give the prospective employer more information regarding aptitudes, general intelligence, interests, and personality. Some college students refer to them as "multiple guess" type questions. Occasionally the interviewer will give you a topic and ask that you write approximately one hundred words on the subject.

Since there is little you can do to prepare for such tests, the only practical suggestion we can make is to recommend that work be accomplished as rapidly and accurately as possible, especially if the test has a time limit. Speed, accuracy, completeness, and your ability to demonstrate how well you can use the English language, or the language you are being tested in, generally figure in determining the final score you attain. If you did not learn how to cope with something like this after having had four years of college, then it is a little late for you to retrace your steps in trying to overcome this deficiency. Employers often refuse to give you the results of such scores. Perhaps a low score can be overcome by being prepared adequately for the interview and having a deep concern about getting the job.

If there is indecision about having the ability and aptitude for a particular field, perhaps the counseling center or vocational testing service on campus can help you. Seeking help of this nature should be done well in advance of your job-seeking venture. The results of the tests you take in a counseling center can best be interpreted by counselors at the center where you took the test.

Some states may require you to take a test displaying your knowledge of the State Constitution or the United States Constitution, or take a national teacher placement test if you are interviewing for a teaching position. This varies from state to state, however.

Various business firms or government agencies give tests that serve their own particular needs.

THINGS YOU SHOULD NOT DO

During the interview you should not:
1. Chew gum or wring your hands.
2. Smoke unless it is suggested you may do so by your interviewer.
3. Argue or discuss personal problems.
4. Blame your grades on your professors.
5. Talk down to or about anyone.
6. Tell hard luck stories.
7. Bluff. This could be your downfall if caught in any semblance of a prevarication.
8. Beg for a job.

THE PERSONAL INTERVIEW

There are several important factors to consider in carrying out the personal interview. These are important to both the employer as well as you. For the employer, the interview serves as a means for judging personal appearance, voice appeal, adaptability, interests, and a means for securing your reactions to living and working conditions and responsibilities. It gives you an opportunity to gain as much information as possible about things pertaining to the particular position for which you are applying, such as the community, living conditions, opportunities for advancement as well as local employment regulations, and salary schedules.

By appearing a little early prior to the interview, you will have time to relax and collect your thoughts. This will permit you to think more clearly. You should go to the interview alone. This is one occasion where your mother, father, a friend, professor or relative cannot help you.

When invited into the interview room, shake hands firmly with the interviewer. Do not use a bone-crusher for a handshake. At the same time a wet-noodle handshake is good only in a noodle factory! If a lady is involved in an interview and extends her hand, a firm grasp with no motion (shaking) should be used. Use the interviewer's name with the prefix — Mr., Mrs., or Miss.

Be poised and relaxed. Do not sit down until the interviewer asks you to be seated. If you cross your legs, do not exaggerate this. This should be done in good taste. While you should be at ease during the interview, omit any unusual mannerisms that you may have and are aware of. As an example, some people continue to button and unbutton their coats, others will twirl a chain around their fingers, fiddle with a piece of jewelry, or keep up a continuous movement of their hands or feet. Things of this nature can become very distracting to one doing the interviewing. Above all, you want to keep the interviewer in a good frame of mind throughout the interview. You want to keep him thinking positively.

Generally, the interviewer will start the conversation with the idea of seeking personal information about you while trying to get you to relax. Gradually he will ease into the job situation. This should help to abate tension and you of all people should know something about YOU!

Look directly at the interviewer, not at the floor or around the room or ceiling. Many people do not realize their glances are indirect, so be conscious of this. If you are going to listen, LISTEN. Good eye-to-eye contact will help you remember all that has been said, whereas, if you look all around the room, you may miss some important fact and the interviewer may think that you are more interested in something else than in getting a job.

Be frank and sincere. Do not exaggerate your qualifications; however, too much modesty gets one no place fast. Do not volunteer information regarding weak areas; however, if this should come out in the conversation, admit it, do not try to hide it, and state what you have been doing to try to correct this deficiency. If you have made some progress in trying to overcome your problem, tell how and why you think you have been successful. This defect could be an area where you have not been properly trained.

It is good to let the interviewer know you are interested in the job; however, do not try to use pressure on him. Being pleasantly persistent is the best approach. If the job is tough to handle, the interviewer might use a "tough" approach to see how you will react to a situation like this; therefore, it is best to keep your composure and show interest until the end of the interview. Be cautious about making up your mind for or against a job until you have had time to assess the situation, unless you are convinced you want the job, if offered. If you would like to have the job, say so. If you are not certain, then ask for some time to think about it before giving a final answer.

Speak at a moderate rate of speed and enunciate clearly. You must be capable of getting your thoughts across in such a manner that they make sense and are comprehensible.

It is best to be careful about discussing religion or politics, unless it is brought up by the interviewer and has something to do with the job. If the job you are interviewing for involves religion or politics, then be prepared to state your feelings accordingly. Sometimes, by discussing these two subjects, they can boomerang if not dealt with carefully.

One of the last things you should talk about is salary and fringe benefits, unless is it brought up by the interviewer. If you mention salary initially and if it is foremost in your mind at the beginning of the interview, the interviewer may think you are more interested in money than in rendering service on the job.

Do not be too aggressive, especially in regard to closing the contract. No matter how favorably impressed the employer may be with you, he may not wish to discuss a contract with you until he has had an opportunity to interview other candidates. Read and make sure all implications regarding the contract are understood before signing it. This lets you know exactly what to expect and it will indicate to the interviewer that you are cautious. This will also let the employer know that you understand what you have signed and that you will not come back later and say, "Well, I did not know I was expected to do this or that."

It is very important to be alert for cues toward the end of the interview as they will give an indication of how the interviewer appraises you. Clarify the next action to be taken and make sure you write down all relevant things such as the name of the interviewer, the name and address of the school district or company, the telephone number and area code. When it is obvious the interview has been completed, leave promptly. Express your appreciation for the interview and once again, utilize the firm handshake.

FOLLOW-UP ACTION

Sometimes follow-up action on your part is necessary to improve the chances of obtaining a definite job offer. Remember, you should be politely persistent, but do not overdo it.

Follow up the interview, if you are interested in the job, with a follow-up letter or a telephone call, by stating briefly the position you were interviewed for and your interest in securing the position. Be prepared for a second interview if necessary.

The follow-up is important because the interviewer might be considering two or three people. If someone else, for example, was offered a job and turns down the offer, this still leaves a job to be filled and the one showing the most initiative and interest will have an inside track in getting the job, if he is properly qualified.

If you are not interested in the job following the interview, then no follow-up action is needed. If a position is offered when it is not desired, it should be turned down immediately by sending a rejection letter to the employer. Keep in mind that courteous action now may lead to a job sometime in the future. Too, it may permit another candidate to actively seek that position.

If employment has not been secured after having made application and being interviewed, try a little harder. Many top-notch people go through five, six or even ten interviews before getting a contract. If you get too discouraged, chances are the next interview will go poorly and this is when the chance of landing a job diminishes. Remember, a positive attitude, a positive effort, and a positive disposition can be your greatest assets when you are being interviewed for a job.

During normal times there will be several people qualified for the same position and an employer cannot hire them all. This is why it is extremely important to be "totally prepared" for that first interview because that may be a most desirable job and it may slip away, not because of lack of qualifications but because you were not ready for the interview.

Keep in mind that although you were not given a position initially, the future may hold a job for you; so always leave a good impression. Never burn a bridge because it may have to be crossed at a later date. Other organizations with good job situations in ideal geographic locations will always have an abundance of applications and it is hard for a new person with little or no experience to break in. So by leaving in good standing and gaining some practical experience with another company, your chances of returning at a later date will be much better if the first try with a large organization is not fruitful. However, this does not mean that a larger company or school district will not hire a beginner.

28

After campus interviews, the employer's representative usually gives the placement staff some indication of the person or persons whose qualifications he is interested in. This information will generally be made available to you by checking with the placement service, and will help you in following up on prospective jobs.

Review the sample formats of various types of letters in the last chapter.

CONTRACTS

A contract is a binding agreement or covenant, usually written between two or more individuals, parties, to do or keep from doing a specified thing, which is enforceable by law.

Remember, the contract you sign should be entered into in good faith by both your employer and yourself. You would not want your employer to break your contract after you signed it; therefore, you should honor it the same as you would want the employing official to honor it. Be aware of all stipulations before signing a contract because an unwanted job generally turns out to be a burden on everyone concerned. Make certain that you want the position before you sign the contract.

Sometimes you have to resign your position for health purposes. If this should occur, it is best to be able to produce a physician's statement to substantiate your contention. You should be aware of any possible health hazards before signing a contract.

THE NEW COMMUNITY

Community adaptability, or the lack of it, is one of the most common causes for the failure of the new employee. It has been said, "When in Rome, do as the Romans do." This is not a situation forced on you; however, it is wise to learn the local power structures in the community. Know both sides of a situation before acting.

Sections of all states and especially nations, in which you have been raised, generally differ a great deal in customs, social and religious backgrounds, as well as outlook on life in general. As a beginning employee you must learn to adapt yourself to the situation and respect the mores of the community or country, even if you are unwilling to accept them as part of a personal philosophy. This does not mean you have to compromise your principles. You should consider the new community "as your own," not just a place of employment. *Never look down on the local citizenry* regardless of the position you may hold. The majority of the members of any given community will ordinarily be patient and act kindly toward you, but their patience should not be taxed to an extreme. You will be respected if your actions deserve respect. There is no way you can force anyone to respect you. This is something you will have to earn. Remember, there is such a thing as a two-way street.

Visit the community before accepting employment if at all possible. If distance does not permit this, perhaps you may know of someone who has lived there or is currently living there. Contact him and ask pertinent questions relative to the community. Another way is to subscribe to the local newspaper or get information from the Chamber of Commerce. You can also contact a clergyman of your faith because he is involved enough in the community to be able to give you an honest appraisal of this new locality. Perhaps your local library or newsstand will carry newspapers that contain information about the area.

WHAT TO DO AFTER SECURING EMPLOYMENT

If a number of letters have been submitted to employing officials, a letter should be sent to them indicating that employment has been found, that you are no longer looking for a job, and thanking them for any consideration they may have given you. Suitable housing should be found in your new locality and you should think about money to move and live on until you get that first paycheck. If you arrange for credit, make sure this is not abused as these monies have to be paid back in addition to paying normal bills. Regardless of when you move from the town you are leaving, make certain all creditors know where you are going and let them know about your new circumstances, for chances are they will be more lenient than they would be if they felt you were leaving town without intending to pay your indebtedness in full. Credit is relatively easy to obtain — it is also easy to lose and is difficult to regain once it is lost. *Treat it with respect.*

SEEKING PROMOTION

Upon entering into a new assignment it is of paramount importance that you perform your job to the best of your ability, because you never know who is observing your work. Oftentimes you may think your efforts are going unnoticed, yet there are many avenues in which your accomplishments can be called indirectly to the attention of your supervisors. Regardless of where you work, employers want results and results speak for themselves. After your employer has watched your work over a period of time and, if a position becomes vacant, he will know if you warrant being considered for promotion and if you are capable of filling their needs.

Sometime, somewhere, almost everyone has had or will have an undesirable job or person to work with regardless of where the job is. One cannot jump up and move every time there is a difference of opinion — the next situation may be worse than the one you left! Remember, there are always two sides to every story. Make sure you know the complete situation and all of the ramifications before suggesting an immediate change that might not work. Ideas are good; however, they must be workable beyond a pad of paper.

If a vacancy occurs and you feel you are both qualified and interested in the position, then make formal application for the opening through official channels. No one should be more interested in your future than you.

Ordinarily, you should remain in a position for a minimum of two years, especially when just working for the first time after graduation, *as this is one of the best recommendations you can have*. Diversely, if your employment record shows seven or eight different jobs over the same number of years, an employer may feel that you are a poor risk, a poor worker, or someone who will move on to another job for almost any reason.

There are exceptions to the rule, however. If you should be offered a promotion after your first year of employment and, if you feel capable of handling the job, then this is reason enough to accept it. Before accepting such a job, it is advisable to consult some competent person that you trust and weigh the pros and cons regarding the job before giving a final answer.

If you receive a promotion, be modest, humble, and accept your advancement and honors with dignity. By showing appreciation and humility your fellow workers will have more respect for you and will be more inclined to follow if you become a leader or supervisor. You should be able to lead as well as follow. Be grateful for your advancement and, *stand tall, walk tall, and think tall!*

FAILURE?

While we have been speaking of promotions and success, how are you going to recognize defeat if and when you meet it for the first time in your life?

Almost every person is bound to meet failure in some form sometime in his life. If you do not meet failure occasionally, then how are you going to recognize defeat when you do meet it? Just because you experience failure and go down does not mean you have to stay down. If you possess sufficient intestinal fortitude, you can overcome temporary defeat. Having had some of these experiences can make you a stronger person, who will be more able to cope with a difficult situation in the future.

Whenever you try to differentiate between defeat and failure, the difference may be this:

To quote a well-known politician, "If you are defeated — *and quit* — you're a failure. But if you are defeated — *and learn* — and if from what you learn you restructure your efforts, gain renewed strength, and use it to come back for another try — you're no failure. You're a success. Success is a man who wished to succeed — and worked. Failure is a man who wished to succeed — and wished."

HIRING A FAMILY?

Interest in the entire family has become an innovative aspect of utmost importance when an employer interviews a prospective employee.

There have been numerous instances where employers request that the husband or wife, and occasionally children, be present during the interview. This approach gives the interviewer an opportunity to see how members of the family react under given conditions. The interviewer is also interested in finding out how the family would adjust to moving to another locality, living in a particular city, state, or country, as well as how they would respond to the breadwinner's working for a particular company.

Poor family relationships often have a drastic influence on work habits as well as production. If you go to work "mad" every day, how much are you really going to accomplish of a positive nature?

Sometimes the interviewer will come to the house of the person being interviewed to see how the yard and house, inside and out, are kept and how the family treats personal belongings. If a person is unorganized at home, what can an employer expect of him/her on the job? There is a difference between such a thing as "clean dirt" and "dirty dirt." Clean dirt does not hurt anyone. Dirty dirt can leave an adverse, lasting impression on the interviewer. The type of books, magazines, and newspapers lying around the house can also reflect on a family both positively or negatively.

Ordinarily, these types of interviews are for people over forty years of age, but they can occur with applicants regardless of the age level. Be prepared for almost anything because the employer is looking for someone who can perform satisfactorily day in and day out.

INNOVATIONS IN JOB PLACEMENT

Within the next few years, do not be surprised if a member of the local college placement service staff is assigned to interview you on video tape. After being completed, these tapes can then be sent to prospective employers to view and screen you without ever seeing you in person. This would preclude many interviewers from having to travel to distant places to interview applicants.

If you are really serious about getting a good job after graduation you should start preparing yourself when you first step foot on your college campus. Academic probation, disciplinary probation and other problems that students incur, appear to be eliminating many applicants from the top job market after they graduate, if they graduate. Video tape and computers will take only that which is fed into them — you will not be able to sell yourself in person unless you have a good record, and this type of record is not established during the final year of your education. It is an accumulative process. If a prospective employer is impressed with your video tape interview, he may want to see and interview you in person.

Why should a company with a multimillion dollar business take a chance on an employee who has a record that is undesirable? With certain fields becoming overcrowded, should a school district or company take a chance on a graduate who has substandard credentials? Qualified people, who really want to work and have a concern for fellow employees and the employing agency, will always be capable of finding jobs; they may have to look a little harder, but the job can be found. The marginal person will find it harder and harder to find desirable employment.

You start molding your character long before you enter college, and carry this standard of conduct with you as you go through college and life. Your decisions, after you graduate from college, will reflect either favorably or unfavorably upon you and the institution you graduated from and represent. Certain undesirable traits have a habit of following you regardless of where you go. It becomes more difficult for you to find a job if you become a chameleon.

A college likes to be proud of its graduates. It will be a challenge for you to be one of its better representatives.

To a young person starting out in life, this can be a cold, cold world when you start to hunt for a job. Life is no bed of roses. By being properly prepared from the beginning, job seeking can be made less difficult. Living can then become more pleasant.

SELF-SERVICE EMPLOYMENT AGENCIES

The British Department of Employment, in North London (England) has opened a self-service employment agency where up to 2,000 job vacancies are listed on cards and placed in a "job supermarket."

People are encouraged to come in and browse around and if they find something in the way of a job that is appealing, they take the card to a receptionist who arranges for a job interview between the parties concerned. Officials say this new approach to filling vacant jobs is well liked and gets results, primarily because lengthy paperwork is not required.

HOW TO HAVE MORE ENTHUSIASM AND SELF-CONFIDENCE

"If you have had sadness or defeat or disappointment — the low spots which occur in life — try to become involved in activity that will eliminate interlocking self-reinforcers when you feel dejected: 1) Be prepared to accept the fact there ARE obstacles, that life is not an easy journey; 2) if the obstacles do come, steel yourself to learn something from them, rather than indulge in self-pity and self-recrimination; and 3) find an outlet for your frustrations,

35

your disappointment, and your pent-up sorrowful feeling," says Hubert Humphrey.

To further illustrate the importance of "How to Gain Self-Confidence by Building Your Opinion of You," Dr. Ann Rubin, Associate Professor of the Graduate School of Education, Barry College, Miami Shores, Florida, teaches a highly successful course in confidence building. She overcame many personal setbacks to gain her Ph.D. degree after eighteen years of studying at night.

In an article published July 2, 1972, in *The National Inquirer*, Dr. Rubin defines self-confidence:

"Self-confidence is a feeling that comes from within you. It is built on how you feel about yourself. The lower your opinion of yourself, the less self-confidence you will have.

"If you want to build your self-confidence, there are some practical steps you can take:

— "Think more of yourself. Believe that you are a worthwhile, valuable human being. People who believe they are good and worthwhile are always self-confident.

— "Choose realistic goals and achieve them. Accomplishing something — no matter how small — makes you feel worthwhile. Success is good for self-confidence.

— "If your goals prove to be unrealistic, learn to adjust them. If you can't accomplish the whole project, readjust and get enjoyment from accomplishing at least part of it.

— "Think positively. Count your successes rather than your failures.

— "Associate with people who are successful, positive and self-confident. You'll soon blend in with them and learn to behave like a self-confident person yourself.

— "Make sure you're in a job that makes you happy. If you're happy with your job, the chances are good that you'll become skilled at it. And knowing you're skilled at something will build self-confidence.

— "Be orderly, productive, hard-working and honest. People will think more of you if you are, and their esteem will build your confidence.

— "Recognize other people's needs and try to supply them. For example, if they need praise, give it. If you do this for others, they will do it for you. And having people who are willing to help you will make you confident in your worth.

— "Avoid people with negative personalities. Some people go through life destroying others, because they are failures themselves and want to bring others down to their level.

— "Make friends. Lack of confidence is often a result of loneliness. If you lock your problems within yourself, you don't stand much of a chance of overcoming them. Talk frankly with a friend or preferably a group of people with whom you share trust.

"Remember, anyone can be confident. But you must first honestly answer the question: 'What do I think of myself?' If the answer is 'Not much,' set as your goal the systematic and continual development of self-esteem."

A CRUEL WORLD

When job hunting you cannot always hit the big time initially unless you are "to the manor born," therefore, you may have to settle for a little less until you are better prepared and have gained valuable experience.

In many cases one of the biggest obstacles you will encounter is the lack of experience in your particular field. There has to be a starting point somewhere for everyone, and unless someone gives you a job you cannot get that needed experience. In many cases, unless you have certain prerequisites, you will not be considered for a job.

Occasionally it will be necssary for you to take a lesser job or an assistantship of some sort in order to gain needed experience. Many employers prefer that you have not less than two years of productive experience on the job with the same organization, before talking about future employment opportunities with their firms.

If you accept a job as an assistant to gain experience, this will provide you with an excellent opportunity to prove your worth and value to the organization. Remember, nothing succeeds like success. By doing your best you will be in line for a good recommendation from your employer. This is of vital importance to you when you start searching for a better job. While you will be seeking a job alone, remember that we all had to have a little help somewhere along the line.

CODE FOR SUCCESS

In setting up a basic set of guidelines for your journey through life, select the vocation that is most congenial to your tastes. Take stock of your own situation. If you dislike your job, find something you like. Life is short enough as it is.

Do not let the horror of the blues overcome you. Fight depression with all your might — or it can destroy your ambition forever. Whenever a negative thought enters your mind, eliminate it immediately. Welcome only positive thoughts of success and filter out the remainder. This takes mental discipline, but you can do it.

Whatever you do of a positive nature, do it with all your might, body, and soul. In looking upward and forward aim high, then work your head off to attain your objective. Selectively work toward attainable goals.

As you proceed, exercise both caution and boldness and rely on your own self, for you are the master of your own destiny. If you depend on others to lead the way, it will get you nowhere; however, all of us need to have help from others occasionally. We are all mortal. Seldom do you ever get a job completely alone. Sometimes it is not what you know, but whom you know. Even though you will need some help, learn to rely on yourself; this can lead you to infinite personal achievements.

In proceeding through life learn something useful and do not put "all of your eggs in one basket." Expand your background of abilities in more than one direction; however, you will want to specialize in something. If you should not be successful in one line of endeavor, be prepared to meet a new challenge. This paradox is part of life.

It is important for you to be systematic — to have the time and place for everything. *You should plan your work and work your plan.* This system should never fail if you stick to it. Without a semblance of organization, you will struggle awkwardly in a maze of half-completed endeavors.

Tactfully, advertise your abilities. If you do not, who will do this for you? Applicants with a good background have nothing to fear but fear itself. One should remember to be politely persistent in pursuing his objective. With this type of attitude, how can you fail?

There is one final point and that is to read a good daily newspaper every day. Remember what Will Rogers used to say? "All I know is what I read in the newspapers." By reading a good newspaper on a daily basis, you keep informed. Almost everything that will be recorded in history can be found in newspapers and magazines. Select your reading materials and read them carefully. Make use of the knowledge you get from them.

TRY HARDER

As M. R. Kopmeyer reports in a recent book about J. Paul Getty, Mr. Getty gave his secret of success in two words: "Try harder!"

Mr. Kopmeyer comments: "Compounded effort is like compound interest — it expands at a terrific rate. Pyramiding your efforts is like pyramiding your profits — the acceleration in your gains is enormous and the total result . . . well, Paul Getty made one and one-half billion dollars!"

Try harder when you are job hunting.

"Diploma Mills"

In searching for success, if you care enough for the result you will almost certainly attain it, if you have the desire.

"DIPLOMA MILLS"

There are many proprietary firms that purport to provide training that will essentially lead to or guarantee employment in a particular field. If you encounter a firm or agency that allegedly is a "correspondence or diploma mill," ask the firm to provide evidence of the success they claim for their program. The credential received should be one that is accepted by practitioners of the profession that relates to the diploma or certificate.

Most reputable firms require that a prospective employee be able to present a credential obtained from an institution that is certified by the profession associated with or in accordance with state laws in which the agency operates.

If there is any doubt about the authenticity of a firm that "cranks" out diplomas in "ten easy lessons" for a small fee, contact the Better Business Bureau, the Chamber of Commerce, the Consumer Protection Association, Regional and/or National Accreditation Agencies, or your State Attorney General for information and advice.

Even though it may take longer and it may be more costly to get a valid credential from a legitimately recognized institution, follow and observe professional ethics in obtaining a diploma or certificate. Participating in false or questionable representation may place your entire future in jeopardy and may cause you to have to "look over your shoulder" the rest of your life. Your career may depend on the path you follow.

JOB AWARENESS

One of the most important developments taking place in college placement is the increased emphasis on vocational counseling and career planning. It is of paramount importance for college students to start thinking about career planning four years prior to graduating from college.

Advance planning can do much to help you when you eventually start hunting for a job. As you plan your career it is important to keep in touch with the "job market." You should be continuously aware of the fields where most jobs are available.

To assist you, empirical reassessments by educational institutions need be made to determine how well college programs prepare students for their roles in society after graduation. Before employing individuals, employers should reevaluate their educational requirements for various positions, because within recent years, too many over-qualified people have been hired to fill vacancies.

While you should be cognizant of curriculum developments in educational institutions, it is incumbent upon the administration of each college campus to improve its manpower planning and forecasting to avoid unnecessary oversupply of graduates in certain fields. You should be continuously advised of the fields in which the greatest and least demands are anticipated.

It is possible for you to keep aware of trends in educational development and future job opportunities. This will assist you in determining what to major in while in college. When planning a career you should remember that the job market fluctuates according to supply and demand. It changes from year to year and from locality to locality.

The ultimate goal for the college graduate and the employer is for educational institutions to produce graduates who are properly prepared for the "outside world."

A man does not know what he can be or do until properly challenged.

41

2

Applying for a Position in Education

THE PLACEMENT SERVICE WILL HAVE A LIST of all teaching vacancies in the state as well as several surrounding states. Check with the placement secretary and make an appointment for an interview with a school district which interests you.

Chances are that the placement service with which you are affiliated will not have all vacancies listed from across the nation. You will have to take the initiative in checking on vacancies in the teaching profession which may be many miles away. The College Placement Annual is one source document that contains advertisements of teaching positions in many states. Check other directories at the end of this chapter regarding other teaching vacancies and related information. To inquire about teaching in foreign countries, contact the Office of Health, Education and Welfare, HEW North Building, 330 Independence Avenue S.W., Washington, D.C. 20201. When searching for information about teaching in one of the many Indian Reservations, write the Department of Interior, Bureau of Indian Affairs, C Street between 18th and 19th Streets N.W., Washington, D.C. 20240.

If a vacancy is called to your attention by a source from outside the Placement Service, then send a letter of inquiry to the school district immediately. If the reply sounds satisfactory, make formal application for the job and ask the placement service to forward your credentials to the school district involved. The more you help the placement service, the more it can help you.

42

APPLYING FOR A TEACHING CERTIFICATE

Everyone teaching in a public school must be certified by the State Department of Education in the state where he is hired to teach. Each state has its own certification laws and standards with which teachers must comply. In addition to their having certain course requirements, there are obligations regarding age, citizenship, health, and perhaps other areas into which you should check. Some states require the passing of a course on the state's history as well as the federal constitution. The common practice is, however, to allow the teacher two or three years in which to make up needed requirements. Many graduates apply for teaching jobs without knowing whether they can be certified in a particular state. A superintendent cannot offer a contract until he is assured that a legal teaching and/or administrative certificate can and will be issued.

Check with your placement service regarding certification in other states. Some states require a transcript of credits while others send forms to be filled out by the records office of the college or university holding your transcript. You can check with the placement service for proper addresses and then write State Departments of Education for specifics regarding certification in a particular state.

It takes time to issue a certificate — generally several weeks. Do not wait until the last minute and get excited because the State Department of Education does not give a speedy reply to your letter. Perhaps it has several hundred similar letters to answer; apply early and avoid the last-minute rush.

When applying for a job in a private school, check certification requirements as conditions vary from state to state.

Certificates cannot and will not be granted until a degree has been awarded; however, a letter of eligibility for a certificate often can be secured from the State Department of Education. You must submit proof of graduation and evidence that all requirements have been met to secure the certificate.

This letter of eligibility could well be your "passport" to a super-intendent who is considering you for a position, so get this letter in early. It will not only indicate interest, but initiative.

These certificates are not transferable from one state to another. If you have taught for several years in one state and anticipate moving to another, it is best to seek out certification standards from that state as soon as possible — five or six months in advance is not too soon.

The placement service or the dean of the college of education will gladly give out information on how to obtain a teaching certificate.

SOURCE INFORMATION FOR EDUCATION MAJORS

An excellent application letter and the most skillfully prepared resume are useless unless they are directed toward carefully selected employers who have the type of position which you are seeking. You should decide whether to place emphasis on geographical location or on the type of school district you prefer, since this decision will determine your approach to source data. If the following references are properly used, they will give you valuable assistance in compiling a list of logical, prospective employers in a locality where you may want to teach.

1. AMERICAN PERSONNEL AND GUIDANCE ASSOCIATION publishes the APGA Placement Service Bulletin which appears four times each year and gives specific information to members who are candidates for new employment opportunities in the field of personnel, guidance and counseling, and to employers who have positions to fill. The APGA Placement Service does *not* recommend candidates to employers nor positions to candidates; it does *not* arrange appointments or interviews. American Personnel and Guidance Association, 1607 New Hampshire Ave. N.W., Washington, D.C. 20009.

2. AMERICAN ASSOCIATION OF COLLEGES FOR TEACHER EDUCA-

TION puts out a directory listing approximately 600 colleges and universities in the United States that are members of the American Association of Colleges for Teacher Education. Each entry gives the name of the institution, the address, the name of its president and its deans. This publication is revised and published yearly. American Association of Colleges for Teacher Education at 1201 16th Street N.W., Washington, D.C. 20036.

3. ASCUS stands for the Association for School, College and University Staffing and gives a preview of the location, offerings, and salaries in many public schools — elementary through college — in the United States. It is published by Field Enterprises Educational Corporation, Merchandise Mart Plaza, Chicago, Illinois 60654.

4. COLLEGE PLACEMENT ANNUAL is an alpha-geographic document which lists 1,800 corporations and government employers seeking college graduates, cooperating placement offices and members of the College Placement Council. The College Placement Council, Inc., 65 East Elizabeth Avenue, P. O. Box 2263, Bethlehem, Pennsylvania 18018.

5. CONTACT FILE: The Placement service maintains an alphabetical file of all employers who have requested assistance from the service in the past, with the name of the school district, the address, and the person to contact.

6. COOPERATIVE COLLEGE REGISTRY is a means of introducing teachers, prospective teachers, and administrative personnel to more than 200 colleges and universities. A candidate's registration is submitted to colleges when qualifications match needs as listed. This service, provided by fourteen Protestant denominations to their related colleges, is free to the registrant and the institution. Member colleges are in pursuit of academic excellence and the maintenance of standards common to all accredited institutions of higher learning. Student enrollment generally ranges between 600 and 2,000, with a few smaller and some larger. Cooperative

College Registry, One DuPont Circle, Suite 10, Washington, D.C. 20036.

7. CRUSADE FOR EDUCATION is published nine times a year and describes professional openings in the United States as well as abroad for teachers, librarians, administrators, and scientists. Also contained is information on undergraduate scholarships, current graduate awards, summer opportunities, teachers' discount services, writing and part-time work. Advancement and Placement Institute, 169 North 9th Street, Brooklyn, New York 11215.

8. GUIDE TO AMERICAN DIRECTORIES is an alpha-geographic listing of most of the known directories in the United States. This is a valuable source for finding and locating directories, regardless of the field or area. B. Klein Publications, Inc., 11 Third Street, Rye, New York 10580.

9. LOVEJOY'S PREP SCHOOL GUIDE lists some 1,800 private, independent boarding, day and special purpose secondary schools in the United States. Entries cover military schools, schools for the handicapped, church-related schools, schools for special students and others. They are listed alpha-geographically and cross-indexed alphabetically by the type of school. Revised and published periodically by Simon and Schuster, Inc., 1 West 39th Street, New York, New York 10003.

10. NATIONAL ASSOCIATION OF STUDENT PERSONNEL ADMINISTRATORS (NASPA) publishes a Placement Bulletin three times a year containing current Candidate Listings and current Job Openings Lists that are related to the area of College Student Personnel Work. NASPA Placement Service, Illinois State University, Norman, Illinois 61761.

11. NEA-SEARCH is a computer-based locator service operated by the National Education Association which helps teachers locate vacancies. Employing schools as well as teachers may use the service. This service covers U. S. Regions, U. S. Sub-regions,

and certain foreign regions. NEA-SEARCH, 1201 16th Street N.W., Washington, D.C. 20036.

12. PATTERSON'S SCHOOLS CLASSIFIED lists approximately 5,500 private schools, special schools, colleges and universities — both private and public, technical, trade and vocational schools. Listed are names of deans and other administrative officials. Institutions are alpha-geographically arranged by state and city and indexed by type in forty-six categories from architecture to osteopathy to technical and trade schools. It is revised and published yearly. Educational Directories, Inc., P. O. Box 199, Mount Prospect, Illinois 60056.

13. SALARIES PAID AND SALARY-RELATED PRACTICES IN HIGHER EDUCATION carries a report on salaries in higher education and presents a full distribution of salaries paid to each rank in each type of institution and salaries paid to all types of administrative officers. Included also are summaries of the status and trends of several practices related to salaries in higher education. National Education Association, 1201 16th Street N.W., Washington, D.C. 20036.

14. SALARY SCHEDULES FOR TEACHERS gives precise information regarding salary schedules for teachers in reporting school systems with enrollments of 6,000 or more, and for selected systems in high-income suburban areas with enrollments of 1,000 or more. Trends in mean minimum and maximum scheduled salaries are given to show the progress being made toward compensating teachers adequately. National Education Association, 1201 16th Street N.W., Washington, D.C. 20036.

15. THE CHRONICLE OF HIGHER EDUCATION is a weekly chronicle of news and features pertaining to higher education. It contains a bulletin board section which is a clearing house for positions wanted and available. The Chronicle of Higher Education, 1717 Massachusetts Avenue N.W., Washington, D.C. 20036.

16. TEACHER PLACEMENT DIRECTORY serves as an aid in teacher placement. It is published yearly. Advancement and Placement Institute, 169 North 9th Street, Brooklyn, New York 11215.

Most professional societies and associations conduct placement operations at their annual national conventions or conferences. Information may be obtained by writing the Executive Secretary of the association concerned.

3

Applying for a Position in Business

THE WORLD OF BUSINESS covers many areas, including accounting, advertising, actuary, business administration, business operation, computer programming, data processing, finance, management, marketing, personnel work, retailing, sales, secretary science,
and teaching.

Those interested in teaching in the field of business should read
the first chapter and this chapter on business as well as the chapter on education.

All of the business areas mentioned are fairly well defined in
themselves; however, two may need more explanation. An actuary
is a person well-grounded in mathematics as well as business; it is
his job to analyze past events and determine what may happen in
the future. A business operation would be the general area in
which you would learn to operate your own business.

All colleges, schools, and departments of business will not offer
these areas as majors or even minors; however, company training
programs can and will take a well-motivated person and train
him for a new area, in many instances, providing he has the aptitude and background.

The University of Tennessee's business placement office conducted a survey of what employers seek in graduates. The twenty
items include: personality, grades, motivation, appearance, ability
to communicate, work experience, maturity, attitude, loyalty, ability to look ahead, extra-curricular activities, decisiveness, willing-

ness to work, business interest, common sense, tact, attendance, alertness, and perseverance.

It is not desirable to accept a position on the spot unless you are convinced this is the job for you. Take a day or two to think it over, covering all facets of the job, the future, and the community. If you think you will be happy with the job, its possibilities and the community, you will do a better job and advance much more quickly than you will if you are unhappy with the job and the community is undesirable for you.

There are three avenues for the job-seeker to follow: 1. Accept the offer and immediately quit seeking another job; 2. Tactfully reject the offer; 3. Seek more time to consider the offer. By all means, discuss the job with your wife or husband.

Being able to accomplish something without constant supervision, being willing to tackle a tough situation and produce good results, and working well with others are things that make for a successful business person.

Throughout the school year the placement service will keep all job-seekers informed about every job opportunity that may fit their job description and/or qualifications. This will vary on a local, regional, or a national basis.

When registering with the placement service, be sure to list work experience and interests, especially if they are outside the major or minor area.

The service will generally have a job opening file which lists alphabetically all business openings. The bulletin boards near the placement office, the department of business administration, or any campus bulletin board might be designated as a place to list job openings.

Become familiar with your school's way of distributing information about jobs and take the initiative to find out and keep yourself informed about campus visitations and/or job listings in the field of business.

SOURCE INFORMATION FOR BUSINESS MAJORS

1. COMPANY LITERATURE FILES are invaluable and the placement service should have an up-to-date file or be willing to assist you in getting pamphlets and brochures from specific companies.

2. STATE AND CITY CHAMBERS OF COMMERCE are always willing to help because they are interested in attracting new ideas and new people to their communities. Larger companies will be listed by name, business and number of employees with the key person to contact, generally, the personnel manager. The contents often vary and in some cases there is a charge for these directories.

3. CAREER SEARCH lists 400 top-rated companies who are searching for executive talent.

4. COLLEGE AND UNIVERSITY BUSINESS contains a Classified Advertising section pertaining to Positions Wanted and Positions Open in mostly business and management related areas at college level such as: Accountant, Administrative Assistant to the President, Architect, Auditor/Systems Analyst, Bookstore Manager, Budget Officer, Bursar, Business Officer, College President, Computer Services Director, Controller, Data Processing Instructor, Dean, Dietitian, Director of Auxiliary Enterprises, Director of Security, ETV Station Manager, Food Service Director, Housemother, Institutional Research Director, Maintenance Director, Vice President/Director of Development, and Vice President for Operations. College and University Business, 230 West Monroe Street, Chicago, Illinois 60606.

5. THE COLLEGE PLACEMENT DIRECTORY contains some 1,500 companies and government agencies hiring U. S. college graduates, information on all levels of government work, cross-indexes of companies and government agencies arranged by types of job opportunities offered and by location. Listed are most U. S. and Canadian colleges plus names of placement directors and other relevant information.

6. THE FOREIGN JOB GUIDE contains some 400 international associations, financial organizations, teacher/school administrator

sources, United States companies with foreign operations, mining companies, shipping companies, government agencies, chambers of commerce, embassies and consulates, and foreign interest associations.

7. A GUIDE TO AMERICAN DIRECTORIES is an alphabetical listing of most of the known directories in the United States. This is a valuable source for finding and locating directories, regardless of the area or field.

8. WHO'S HIRING WHO has 50,000 current job openings listed, where they are, how to apply, summer job openings, training opportunities for senior applicants, executive jobs above $25,000, numerous free job-market services for applicants as well as employers.

9. MOODY'S INVESTORS SERVICE provides a complete financial picture of American and foreign corporations engaged in the world of business. It gives a general description of the company such as history, size, offices, the names of officers and directors. This service is divided into five volumes as follows:

Moody's Banks and Finance
Moody's Industrials
Moody's Municipals and Governments
Moody's Public Utilities
Moody's Transportation

10. POOR'S REGISTER OF DIRECTORIES AND EXECUTIVES is a list of some 20,000 American and Canadian corporations, giving the company name and address, principal products, number of employees, and the names of important officers and directors. This register also lists, alphabetically, prominent persons in industry, giving a brief sketch of each individual. This sketch includes his business affiliation, office and home address, education, fraternal affiliation, age and birthplace.

11. THOMAS' REGISTER OF AMERICAN MANUFACTURERS comes in four volumes. Volumes 1 and 2 list U. S. manufacturers in a particular industry and give locations of these industries as well as capi-

tal ratings. Volume no. 3 lists, alphabetically, the manufacturers, with home offices, branches, affiliations, succeeding concerns, cable addresses, and other relevant information. Also included is a trade name index which identifies the manufacturer of a product by its trade name. Volume no. 4 is a product index-finding guide keyed to Volumes 1, 2 and 3.

OTHER DIRECTORIES

12. BEST'S INSURANCE REPORTS are reports which are divided into three volumes: Life, Fire and Casualty, Surety and Miscellaneous. These reports provide a complete financial picture of all insurance companies, their history, address, investment data, and information on the management and operational procedures. This information is very similar to that covered in *Moody's Banks and Finance.*

13. GUIDE TO AMERICAN BUSINESS DIRECTORIES lists individual trade directories compiled by the United States Department of Commerce. They are indexed according to the nature of industries, their key men, their products, allied fields, and sources of material.

14. THE FORTUNE DIRECTORY lists the 500 largest U. S. Industrial Corporations.

15. WHO'S WHO IN COMMERCE AND INDUSTRY is a series of short biographies of living men and women who are prominent in the business world. These are listed alphabetically and go into more detail than *Poor's Register.*

16. WHO'S WHO IN TRANSPORTATION AND COMMUNICATION is another series of biographies of individuals who work in the fields of transportation and communication.

17. DIRECTORY OF AMERICAN FIRMS OPERATING IN FOREIGN COUNTRIES covers some 3,500 American corporations controlling and operating more than 9,000 foreign business enterprises.

4

Applying for a Government Job

CHALLENGING GOVERNMENT PROGRAMS CONSTANTLY CALL for talented men and women. These programs are of critical importance to the American people and can succeed only through the skilled performance of creative professionals in many fields. Here is an opportunity for you to play a significant part in the governmental affairs of the future. Through your nearest City Employment Office, State Department of Employment, Post Office, and other sources listed, you have an opportunity to check into and enter into a career with a level of government of your choice, after becoming properly qualified by passing written and/or oral examinations, and by meeting other standards as specified by the employing agency.

There are government jobs at local, state, and national levels, though many of us think of only the "national level" when we hear government positions mentioned. The national level, however, offers many more opportunities, and the state ranks second, and the local level generally is limited unless it is in a large city.

The national government provides more career opportunities. Their general service (GS) ratings run from 1 to 18. Check the latest publications for salaries listed according to ratings, along with related fringe benefiits. Local post offices have federal government publications or they can tell you how to secure them.

Most jobs will require some type of examination, regardless of its level. The examination for entry into a federal job is perhaps the most rigorous. It is said that these examinations are often failed due to lack of knowledge in taking examinations, rather than the lack of knowledge of what is actually contained in the test.

Many college and university book stores and newsstands have study booklets for such tests. The ARCO publication on "Federal Service Entrance Examinations" is an excellent one to study. It is unlikely the study booklet will contain actual questions contained in the test; however, it will list the types of questions and since these tests are timed, the study booklet will help one to practice pacing and budgeting time as well as learning what to expect on the test. The booklet contains sample tests and these often point out weak areas that can be overcome before taking the actual test.

About twenty-five percent of all jobs with the federal government exist in the Washington, D.C., area and the remaining seventy-five percent are spread out across the nation and throughout the world. In most cases, the job-seeker must accept a position that is open and has little choice of geographical location; however, once experience has been gained moves are permitted.

Every state has at least one federal job information center. Some have several. The District of Columbia and Puerto Rico also have such centers. Information on current job openings plus information about taking required examinations can be secured from these centers.

The college graduate with no previous experience can usually expect to enter the general service at a 5 to 7 level, whereas the person with a master's degree and some experience can enter as high as the 7 to 9 level. This will vary with the degree of experience.

"Mid-level" positions are classified from 9 to 12 and a person with five years experience, three of which can include obtaining a bachelor's degree, can enter at the 9 level and an additional year of experience is required for the 10 to 12 level.

The "senior-level" includes ratings 13 to 15 and generally has executive-type people with six or more years experience. The "super grade" includes ratings from 16 to 18 and these people are generally in policy-making and appointive type positions.

Each GS rating has ten built-in promotional steps. There is little limit on promotion; however, from grades 1 to 5 no more than two promotions are permitted a year. Well-qualified college graduates may get "double promotions," that is, jump from 5 to a 7 level, from 7 level to a 9 level, and a 9 level to a 11 level. From then on only single jumps are permitted.

Benefits of federal employment include the ability to move between agencies or within the same agency for which you qualify without reexamination. Annual leave (vacation) for the first three years is thirteen working days, twenty days for three to fifteen years, and twenty-six working days for all over fifteen years of experience.

There are eight paid holidays each year, a liberal sick leave policy, government-shared cost on medical insurance, injury compensation, and a joint contributory system for retirement. Term life insurance may be purchased at a nominal rate.

Those required to register under the Selective Service Act will still be considered for employment. If you join the service voluntarily, you will have reemployment rights with the government upon discharge from the service. Salary increases go on even though you are in the service; so it is possible to return at a higher grade than when you left.

Applications are kept on file for a year. Unless employment with the federal government is secured the first year, a new application must be submitted. It is advisable to fill out one extra copy of everything when making that first application and keep one in a safe place to use for quick reference if another has to be submitted.

Jobs most often filled at the "mid-level" 9 to 12 ratings, include contract negotiator, loan specialist, public information specialist, writer-editor, investigator, equal employment officer, veteran claims examiner, personnel specialist, and management analyst.

Actual job experience must be in the job area or closely related. For instance, a college graduate could not expect to count sales-clerk experience for a highly specialized position, as far as rating purposes go.

The "senior-level" positions with GS ratings of 13 to 15 generally call for backgrounds in administration, technical services, staff services, management, and professional services. Openings at this level are usually termed "critical" and all applications are welcomed.

Related experience for the 13 to 15 levels might include sales, sales management, military personnel administration, construction, retail trade, mining, building and equipment maintenance, as well as manufacturing techniques.

At this level, your background and education must demonstrate that you are capable of performing at the administrative, supervisory, managerial, staff or professional work level with a high degree of responsibility.

APPLYING FOR FEDERAL JOBS

Send all correspondence to:

  Desk 408
  U.S. Civil Service Commission
  Washington, D.C. 20415

Submit two copies of Standard Form 171 only, unless directed otherwise. Do not send printed resumes, awards, commendations, professional papers, transcripts or photos. Send one card, Form 5001-ABC, with your application. Complete Standard Form 15 if claiming five- or ten-point veteran preference. Documentary proof must be submitted when claiming the veteran preference which permits five or ten points to be added to the score of the examination.

There are more than two thousand job classifications at the federal level and it is advisable for those interested to read specific job classification pamphlets as well as general pamphlets explaining federal jobs in more detail. Pamphlet no. 4 will give a general overview and by relating area-interests to a staff member in the job information centers, more specific information can be obtained.

SOURCE INFORMATION FOR GOVERNMENT JOBS

1. CAREERS IN ATOMIC ENERGY reveals statistics on programs in atomic energy, available positions, part- and full-time; graduate research contracts or technical jobs in colleges and universities, hospitals, research institutions and the government. U. S. Printing Office, Division of Public Documents, Washington, D.C. 20402.

2. CAREERS IN ENGINEERING, MATHEMATICS, SCIENCE are three fields of demand as the booklet on "Careers in Engineering, Mathematics, Science and Related Fields" points out. This booklet lists more than 385 free and inexpensive publications discussing careers in science, agriculture, biological science, engineering, forestry, health professions, mathematics and the physical sciences. U. S. Office of Education in Washington, D.C. or the U. S. Printing Office, Division of Public Documents, Washington, D.C. 20402.

3. CAREER OPPORTUNITIES AS A FOREIGN SERVICE OFFICER decribes opportunities in the foreign service of the U. S. Government; how to qualify as an officer in the service; work and training of officers; pay and promotions; allowances, leaves, benefits. U. S. Printing Office, Division of Public Documents, Washington, D.C. 20402.

4. SENIOR LEVEL POSITIONS (GS-13, 14, 15). These positions are used by federal agencies to fill high-level administrative, management, staff, and technical service positions in Washington, D.C., throughout the United States, and in foreign countries. U. S. Printing Office, Division of Public Documents, Washington, D.C. 20402.

5. FEDERAL SERVICE ENTRANCE EXAMINATION (GS-5 through GS-7). This examination is designed primarily as an avenue through which young people with promise may enter the federal

service. If you have a college education or equivalent experience, this examination offers many oportunities. Those of you who qualify will be considered for a wide variety of career fields in over fifty federal agencies and in various geographical locations. Over 200 kinds of positions are filled through this one examination. It is, in effect, one application to many employers at the same time. Federal establishments make several thousand appointments each year from this one examination to career positions located in Washington, D.C., and throughout the United States. A limited number of overseas positions are also filled from this examination. The federal service offers excellent opportunity for advancement through its Merit Promotion Program if you demonstrate potential capability for high-level responsibility and leadership. United States Civil Service Commission, Washington, D.C. 20415.

6. LOCAL AND REGIONAL CIVIL SERVICE EXAMINATIONS OFFERING THE BEST JOB OPPORTUNITIES, (AN2280). U. S. Civil Service Commission, Washington, D.C. 20415.

7. MID-LEVEL POSITIONS (GS-9 through GS-12). The number of specific jobs filled varies considerably from location to location, but on a nationwide basis these are examples of the more commonly filled jobs that do not require tests: Contract Negotiator, Loan Specialist, Public Information Specialist, Writer-Editor, Investigator, Equal Employment Officer, Veterans Claims Examiner, Personnel Specialist, and Management Analyst.

Many Government jobs in grades GS-9, GS-11, and GS-12 are covered under more specific announcements. They are: Accountant/Auditor/Internal Revenue Agent, Air Traffic Controller, Agricultural/Biological Sciences, Computer Specialist, Engineering/Physical Sciences/Mathematics, Librarian, Nurse, Psychologist, Social Worker/Correctional Treatment Specialist, and Teacher. If your education and experience is in one of these fields, you should apply under that announcement.

Some positions have specific educational and professional requirements — usually a major in the particular field plus two or more years of professional experience or graduate study — and no written test is required. These specific positions are: Anthropologist, Archaeologist, Economist, Educational Advisor/Program Specialist/Services Officer, Foreign Affairs/International Relations Officer, Geographer, Historian/Archivist, Manpower Analyst, Museum Curator, Public Health Educator, Social Science Analyst/Program Specialist, Sociologist, and Urban Planner. (In all of the jobs, except Economist and Urban Planner, only a few vacancies occur each year.) If you are qualified for any of the positions shown above, you may apply without having to take the written test. However, you will be considered *only* for these positions, and cannot receive consideration for any other positions filled through this announcement. You must take the written test to be considered for positions other than those listed above. Mid-Level Desk, U. S. Civil Service Commission, Washington, D.C. 20415.

8. OCCUPATIONS, PROFESSIONS AND JOB DESCRIPTIONS (PL33A). Superintendent of Documents, Washington, D.C. 20402.

9. TEACHING OPPORTUNITIES in the United States and foreign colleges, public and private schools, summer jobs and certification requirements plus information on teacher supply and demand and salaries. U. S. Government Printing Office, Division of Public Documents, Washington, D.C. 20402.

10. TEACHING OPPORTUNITIES, A DIRECTORY OF PLACEMENT INFORMATION (OE-26000-64). U. S. Office of Education Circular 737: 1-25 '64, United States Office of Education, Washington, D.C.

Applications will be accepted from students who expect to complete, within nine months, appropriate graduate work which would permit them to meet the qualification requirements.

The federal government, like most private companies, fills most vacancies for experienced personnel through promotions of present employees. Consequently, most new employees are at the lower grade levels.

About twenty-five percent of the jobs filled from the MID-LEVEL
POSITIONS announcement are with agencies located in the Washington, D.C., Metropolitan Area. Although a very limited number
of appointments have been made overseas, the vast majority —
about seventy-five percent — have been made in locations throughout the country, outside the Washington, D.C., area. Most jobs
are in the larger metropolitan areas.

STATE CIVIL SERVICE

Each of the fifty states differs in its civil service type of arrange-
ment. The thing they have in common is that dismissal without
good reason is prohibited.

Generally required are the applicant's having an address within
the state of application, the applicant's having a valid driver's
license in that state, an automobile registered in that state, and
eligibility to vote. Some things are waived if the job is critical;
however, it is best to check with the particular state. Some requirements vary from state to state. Contact the state employment
office for information about state civil service jobs.

State, local and federal jobs have wage scales similar to industry
today so they get and keep good personnel. A steady job, growing
seniority and fringe benefits are things that are attracting well-
qualified personnel into civil service jobs today.

Many cities and towns have civil service jobs that are operated
in a manner similar to the state and national level which insures
their getting good personnel, giving them an opportunity to earn
a good living.

There are several reasons a person can be dismissed from his
job; however, the reason must be a bona fide one and not just
because the "boss" dislikes him.

5

Employment and Schooling for Veterans

IF YOU ARE IN THE MILITARY SERVICE and are not approaching eligibility for retirement, think twice before leaving the service to return to civilian life. Too often servicemen have thought that the grass looked greener on the other side of the fence, and requested separation from the service. Many of them felt that someone out in the business world was just waiting for them with open arms. This probably is true for those who have something special to offer. Too many of those without a special skill have found that some people in society forget quickly that you served your country in a military capacity. There are not many employers who are ready to offer you something on a silver platter, unless you can produce for them. The inability to find appropriate work has caused many ex-servicemen to return to active duty with a military organization. There you can earn a comfortable salary while learning a trade, and can enjoy many extra privileges such as getting a college degree, in addition to serving your country. At the end of twenty-plus years in the service, you can retire with a healthy monthly income and still be entitled to many fringe benefits. Remember that a break in service hinders future promotion. Again, think twice before leaving the service.

Each year, however, many thousands of men and women leave the military service after serving one or more terms or after twenty or more years after which they retire with a pension. In some cases, these people retire early with a medical discharge.

If you anticipate leaving the military service you should plan well in advance of the actual date of separation. Some veterans will want to enter or reenter institutions of higher learning under the G. I. Bill; others will be seeking jobs for the first time; and others will return to jobs they held before entering the service.

If you are applying for entry into a technical training school, junior college, college or university, do so at least six months in advance of anticipated enrollment so you will have time to handle all of the necessary paper work before you enter the educational institution. Choose three or four colleges to which to submit applications, to insure that one of them will admit you on time. Your base educational officer can help advise you. In making application to these colleges, find out which ones accept credit earned in military schools. This will vary from college to college. If one of them will accept military credit, it can save you much time, effort, and money in the future if you elect to go to that particular college.

For those veterans returning to former jobs, write your employer and tell him your anticipated date of discharge and the date you will be available.

Veterans applying for a full-time job for the first time or those retiring from military service after twenty years will have to be better prepared. Letters of application, resumes, letters of recommendation and other needed references will have to be prepared. See the appendix for samples.

The Department of Defense has a training program entitled "Transition Program," to provide maximum guidance and training or educational opportunities to servicemen during their last six months of active duty to prepare them for reentry into civilian life.

This Transition Program operates on a decentralized basis at more than 200 bases in the Air Force, Army, Marines, and Navy. Most of these training sites are located inside the United States and six months before being discharged, servicemen fill out a questionnaire to determine interest in this voluntary program.

The Referral Program

The scope of this program has four basic elements: counseling, skill training, education, and placement. Priority in this program is given to enlisted personnel who were combat disabled, are ineligible for reenlistment, had entered the service with no civilian job experience and did not acquire a civilian-related skill while on active duty, have served almost exclusively in the combat type military specialties, and those with low educational achievement.

When possible, training and attention will be devoted to those in the following categories: those wanting to upgrade their military skills which are civilian-related, those needing refresher training in civilian skills learned prior to being in the service, retirees wishing to obtain a useful civilian skill, and those needing assistance to gain civilian job information about the use of their military acquired skills.

State employment agencies can help in acquiring jobs for veterans, and there is no charge for their service. Some commercial employment agencies often charge high fees for their services, and some offer a resume preparation service. Be aware of what you will be required to pay and how it must be paid, if you use a commercial agency.

THE REFERRAL PROGRAM

The objective of the Referral Program is to help career servicemen and women move into a meaningful second career in civilian life through improved counseling and the aid of computer technology.

Other objectives include providing improved means of communication between prospective employers and servicemen retiring after twenty to thirty years of duty. Generally between the ages of forty-one to fifty-one, servicemen are still young enough to have saleable skills that are needed.

This service is available six months after discharge or for one year in the case of a service-connected disability. Once you have secured a job through the Referral Program, your name is removed from the list and you are no longer eligible for assistance.

64

Information secured from the retiree is matched with information from prospective employers through the use of a computer. To get maximum benefit, a retiree should negotiate all paper work and counseling six months before retirement.

Additional information about the Referral Program may be secured from the Referral Program Coordinator, OASD (M&RA), MR&U, The Pentagon, Washington, D.C. 20301.

RETIRED MILITARY PERSONNEL IN FEDERAL JOBS

Since December 1, 1964, retired members of the uniformed services may be appointed to any job with the Federal Government for which they are qualified, except that retired regular component military officers are subject to Dual Compensation Laws. Other retired members must meet any civil service requirements which include taking an examination, if required, and make a high enough score so they will rank among the best qualified for the openings. Check Personnel Management Series No. 21 of the Bureau of Policies and Standards of the U.S. Civil Service Commission, Washington, D.C. 20415, for further details.

EMPLOYMENT AFTER SERVICE

For reemployment rights with the same employer, a veteran must have five years or less of active duty before the employer is obligated to rehire him at his old job or one similar to it. The veteran must apply for the old job within ninety days of discharge or within a year in the case of extended hospitalization. National Guardsmen with three to six months duty must reapply for the old job within thirty-one days after separation. If trouble is encountered with a former employer, contact the nearest Office of Reemployment Rights, Department of Labor. If an office cannot be located contact the U.S. Department of Labor, Labor-Management Services Administration, Office of Veterans Reemployment Rights, Washington, D.C. 20210. This same office supplies a "Veterans' Reemployment Rights Handbook," which is designed to assist those who are concerned with the reemployment rights of veterans.

If a federal job was held prior to entering the service, you may return and expect to come back at a higher rate of pay than when you left.

When a veteran returns to civilian life and is unable to find employment immediately, he or she is eligible for unemployment benefits. Local state employment agencies can help the veteran to fill out the proper papers for unemployment compensation.

There are several pamphlets and brochures a veteran will want to read and keep for references purposes. They include: "Federal Benefits for Veterans and Dependents," VA fact sheet, 1s-1; "Your Personal Affairs," DOD PA-6A; and "Once A Veteran," DOD PA-5A. U. S. Government Printing Office, Washington, D.C. 20415.

THE RETIRED OFFICER

The Employment Clearing House provides personal counseling and assistance in preparing all personal data for retired officers or prospective retirees, regardless of the branch of the service.

A lot of retirees really need a fresh breath — a change — but too many want to cling to the same old type of job. In most cases that ends when you hang up your uniform. Many are actually scared to get out of that "rut" and start something new.

In many instances, retirees turn down excellent offers because they are waiting for a job for which they are better qualified. They are really waiting for jobs like the ones they had in the service. Unfortunately, there are not too many opportunities for a platoon leader in civilian life.

Psychiatrists counseling retirees have found that "false pride" is the greatest stumbling block a retiree has to overcome, especially among officers. The higher the rank the officer has at retirement the more false, or inflated pride, he may have.

By being realistic and honest with yourself, you can land a

rewarding job that will bring in extra money as well as providing personal satisfaction.

As a retired officer you want to remember that you have received illimitable training in various areas that can be of paramount importance to you in a new job if applied properly. Many of the things you learned are not taught in civilian life. You need to have the power to recall and know when and how to use these skills judiciously.

The Employment Clearing House can provide its service by mail, telephone, or during a personal visit to its office. The personal visit is advantageous because counseling can be provided and the retiree can look over all of the jobs currently available and can choose the places to send resume and credentials.

Officials at the Employment Clearing House (ECH), in most cases, get complete job descriptions so the job-seeker will know what he is applying for.

It is important for you, once you have a job, to notify the ECH and request they keep your records current. Sometimes applicants accept temporary employment and in these cases, they should request that their files be kept active.

Also, it is important when using the ECH service to keep your files up-to-date, especially as far as address, telephone number and job objective is concerned. In some cases additional education or training will widen your scope and this information must be relayed to the ECH if a maximum effort is to be expected from their placement services.

Employment Clearing House
The Retired Officer's Association
1625 Eye Street N.W.
Washington, D.C. 20006
Telephone: 202/783-8755

GOING INTO BUSINESS

The Small Business Administration is anxious and willing to give

Caution

counseling to any retired military person wishing to start his own business. The SBA calls on the Service Corps of Retired Executives (SCORE) to provide counseling, advice and analysis of the complete situation.

Hopefully, people will seek this help before starting a business; however, this is not always the case. SCORE offers a wide range of business, scientific or management expertise and in-office assistance is free. There are more that 150 SCORE chapters across the nation and any Small Business Administration can be of help.

Some pitfalls for those starting out in business for the first time include lack of operating capital to insure giving the business every possible chance of success, lack of accounting and bookkeeping, not studying the market and most of all — not having a basic knowledge about business.

Always check with the Better Business Bureau, the Consumer Protection Association, and your banker before putting your money into any type of dealership, franchise, or distributorship. Additionally, it is also advisable to talk to several local businessmen to see if your particular business will already have a market or if a market will have to be built. Taking steps such as these can be of much benefit to you before starting out on a business venture.

CAUTION

It is advisable for a retired military man *not* to use military terminology and/or experience when talking, writing letters or in making up his resume. Some people do not understand military terms and may resent your placing too much emphasis on your service record. *Handle this situation wisely.*

6

40-Plus Job Seekers

ACCORDING TO A DEFINITION in the *Random House Dictionary of the English Language,* "a Renaissance Man is a present-day man with many broad interests who has the opportunity to indulge himself in them so as to acquire a knowledge of each that is more than superficial." The same can be said today of a Renaissance Woman in the twentieth century.

Some people are "old" at 40 and others are "young" at 70 which leads you to believe that "old age" is simply a state of mind. Some people do their best work late in life and in many cases, the older you are, the more successful you become.

For example, Grandma Moses, at the age of 78, began to paint for pleasure and she was entirely self-trained and learned by experimenting.

Albert Einstein is best known for his theory of relativity which completely revised existing concepts of fundamental, universal laws and paved the way for the atomic age. In March 1953, at 74 years of age, he succeeded in devising a single mathematical formula which includes the laws of gravitation, electromagnetism and relativity. These accomplishments are among many other notable contributions he made to the field of physics.

At 78 years of age, Albert Schweitzer was awarded the Nobel Peace Prize in 1952. Prior to this time he was a medical missionary, philosopher, theologian, and musician. At the age of 36 he received his medical degree. Two years later he sailed for Gabon,

French Equatorial Africa, to set up a native hospital at Lambaréné, where he remained a medical missionary the rest of his life.

George Washington Carver was an agricultural chemist, an educator, and was renowned as a world-famous scientist. For his contributions to society he was elected a member of the Royal Society of Arts in London, England, in 1917; in 1939 he received the Roosevelt medal; in 1940 at the age of 76, with his life's savings of $33,000, Dr. Carver established a research foundation bearing his name at Tuskegee Institute, Tuskegee, Alabama.

Other major achievements and recognized work have been recorded for the following people after they were considered past their prime production age. Cervantes completed *Don Quixote* when he was almost 70, Goethe's dramatic poem *Faust* was completed when he was 82, Verdi composed *Othello* and *Falstaff* when in his 70s, George Bernard Shaw was 67 when he wrote *St. Joan,* and The American Red Cross was founded by Clara Barton at age 59. WHAT WILL YOU DO?

It has been said that when some people feel like working they sit down until the feeling goes away, and that others occasionally sit on a tack and complain because it hurts, but will not exert enough energy to get off of it. Then, there are some that look at a situation and picture a completed job, regardless of age. These people think of many ways to paint a picture and still get a good-looking finished product every time. Have you ever heard it said that when you want something done look for a busy man?

There is an old ethic that a man who doesn't work and isn't productive isn't happy. Too often we tell older people to sit down and rest when they have been working all of their lives and want to continue doing so.

40-PLUS CLUBS

Many of the larger cities across the nation have "40-Plus Clubs" for men over forty years of age with executive experience who have earned salaries in five figures for most of their recent working years. These clubs have been highly successful in finding employment for their members.

The chairman of the counseling committee of the 40-plus organization of Washington, D.C., feels the resume is of prime importance for those men over forty. It is prepared in a special way.

For those 40-plus, the resume contains no "job objective" as is characteristic in most resumes. These members sell themselves on their performance records, not on what they think they want to be. The major title describes the type of position the applicant is capable of handling.

The first paragraph of the resume expands on the major title and gives the reader an understanding of the type of industry, or job, you have been involved in plus a generalized thumbnail sketch of you. This is called a "profile."

Supporting the profile will be short paragraphs giving specific accomplishments. Action verbs should be used in the description as this points out that the applicant is a "doer" and not simply someone who attends conferences and is a "buck-passer." Past accomplishments are the key to building the profile resume.

Dates are never shown because this is a giveaway as to age. This can be a barrier in employment despite the Age Discrimination Law.

A one-page resume is most appealing to the majority of employers. Additional pages become cumbersome to read and this can cause rejection when it comes to screening the applicants for the job. A lengthy resume might make the employer feel that it will take too much money to hire you. The trick is to create interest!

Personnel in the 40-plus clubs say there is no rigid format to be used for the resume. Various techniques to attract attention can be used: capital letters, underlining key things, dashes, headlines, reverse indention of paragraphs and occasionally using colored paper. Regardless of which type of format is used, the contents should be neat and orderly.

Ordinarily these types of resumes can be made up rapidly and sent quickly to prospective employers for a specific job. If you are qualified in several fields of work, you can make resumes for each area.

The 40-Plus Club of Washington, D.C., sends out forty-five to fifty word paragraphs on its members to prospective employers who ask for a person's file by number — no name mentioned. Here is one extreme caution you should take when applying for a job. If you answer an ad blindly in a trade magazine, newspaper or pamphlet, it may be your current employer advertising for help!

Non-profit organizations, such as the 40-Plus Club, take pride in their sending responsible employees out for an interview. They screen applicants closely before they are accepted for membership.

Active members must attend weekly general meetings and contribute at least one day a week to the operation of the organization.

ADDRESSES FOR 40-PLUS CLUBS

CHICAGO, ILLINOIS
40-Plus, Inc. of Chicago
343 South Dearborn
Chicago, Illinois 60603

CINCINNATI, OHIO
40-Plus Club
P.O. Box 2033
Cincinnati, Ohio 45201

DENVER, COLORADO
40-Plus Club
14 East 14th Avenue
Denver, Colorado 80204

LOS ANGELES, CALIFORNIA
40-Plus Club
672 South Lafayette Park Place
Los Angeles, California 90057

PHILADELPHIA, PENNSYLVANIA
40-Plus Club
1716 Chestnut
Philadelphia, Pa. 19103

OAKLAND, CALIFORNIA
40-Plus Club
1990 Embarcadero
Oakland, California 94606

WASHINGTON, D.C.
40-Plus Club
810 18th Street
Washington, D.C. 20002

It is advisable to telephone for an appointment prior to visiting the club. The advisors will inform you of their methods of operation and what is expected of you if you intend to participate in their program.

SELF-RELIANCE

Do not rely too much on friends, co-workers or anyone else who you feel will go out and get a job for you. Tell those you know that you are looking for a job. Do not sit back and wait for them to act. You act!

Getting interviews on your own will take initiative, persistence, time and effort. It can be done if you know how to proceed. One way is to check the yellow pages of your telephone directory to get the name of companies that you might be interested in working for. Ask for either the Personnel Department or the Supervisor of Employment. They will be in a position to give you the necessary particulars.

Through this method many people can secure a job on their own. Organize your thoughts and make a concentrated effort to land a job. Never get discouraged because there will be some "no's," some employers will say "maybe"; then sooner or later, that job will come.

While job-hopping is not advocated unless you can definitely improve your position, job-hoppers are used to "scrapping" for a job whereas career-type people have come to gain a feeling of security and take their jobs for granted. The scrapper, through experience, often is better qualified to hunt for a new job and keep going whereas a person who has been on a job for ten to fifteen to twenty years will easily get discouraged and panic when he is out of a job. Take time out to organize yourself and plan on how you will seek another job. Do not be afraid to take a temporary job. Many engineers have wound up working in repair shops, teachers have been teacher aides, and salesmen have worked in gasoline

73

stations. People with this kind of determination are keeping the bills paid until they get the job they have been looking for.

Answering want ads in newspapers and trade publications can often land good jobs. Do not be afraid to let it be known that you are looking for a job and do not be afraid to respond to a job that does not exactly fit your background.

Above all, keep busy. Make job hunting your current full-time job. Perhaps the hardest job in the world, when you are accustomed to working, is "looking" for a job. This will demand as much energy and planning as any work project you have ever carried out. Write letters of inquiry pertaining to jobs, help friends find employment, and do not feel sorry for yourself. After hearing so many "no's," it is easy to become discouraged and give up — never let this happen to you. Do not give up until you have landed that job.

Look listed these important items for the job seeker in its May 18, 1971, issue: The resume, employment agencies, getting the interview on your own, answering want ads, the interview, never doubting yourself and your ability, being prepared to change job direction, not relying too much on friends or co-workers, and most of all keeping in the pursuit of a job.

JOB MARKET VARIABLES

In the job markets of the United States, there are several variables that have had, and will continue to have, profound influence on the employment of older workers, according to a recent report by the National Institute of Industrial Gerontology, the National Council of the Aging in cooperation with the U.S. Department of Labor's Manpower Administration.

Some of the most important factors include:

1. The general economic conditions. An economy growing sufficiently rapidly to utilize the productive capacity of the nation, including its human resources, is essential if older workers are to hold the jobs they have and find others when they are displaced.

Rapid growth per se, however, does not assure full use of all older people who would like to work. Without growth, their condition, like that of other groups, would be worsened.

2. The existence of openings for older workers is not enough to assure their employment. They must be sufficiently able, adaptable, mobile and flexible to take advantage of these openings. Sometimes older workers have special problems in adjusting to changes in the job market.

3. Additional openings for older workers and for other groups can sometimes be created only at the price of inflation. Furthermore, there are limits beyond which further increases in general demand will not increase employment appreciably, if job specifications and worker qualifications do not match.

4. Older workers already employed in growth industries are likely to be retained on their jobs or shifted to others they can fill. However, openings in rapidly growing manufacturing industries are likely to be filled by young workers or with women.

5. Retention of a large proportion of older workers in some industries is not a reliable indication of where older workers can find jobs because higher average age within the work force may be an indication of declining employment in that industry.

6. The acceptability of older workers to employers depends on their relative productivity, adaptability and mobility compared with other available workers. Competition from both groups has been increasing and it appears likely to continue.

7. For a variety of reasons older workers are less mobile geographically and occupationally than young people. This tends to restrict reemployment possibilities once they become unemployed.

8. Low unemployment rates among older workers may not indicate full employment but rather may reflect withdrawal from those who cannot find work.

9. The "older worker" group is not homogenous or static. Any experienced worker who has trouble finding a job primarily because of age constitutes an older worker problem. The numbers

75

and characteristics of such workers have varied considerably in the past and may be expected to do likewise in the future. The principal objective here is to sort out the variables that will determine the future dimensions of older worker employment problems.

Full use of the nation's human resources would require that people of any legal working age who are able and willing to work, be able to find employment suitable to their abilities. Only during World War II did such a situation exist. The person who does the best job of "selling" his abilities and capabilities will stand a better chance of landing a job. Each year we have more and more older people in the forty to fifty-four and fifty-five to sixty-four age groups and in many instances, they need the work because Social Security and/or retirement pay is not enough for them to live on.

It is important for America to keep the production of goods and services growing at a rate which will fully utilize the nation's capacity of human resources on the job.

SENIOR AIDES

The National Retired Teacher's Association/American Association of Retired Persons is working with a project called "Senior Aides," and operates in Atlanta, Georgia; Cleveland, Ohio; Jacksonville, Florida; Kansas City, Missouri; Louisville, Kentucky; and St. Petersburg, Florida.

This organization recruits, trains people for jobs, finds employment for its enrollees and also helps other people fifty-five-and-over find jobs. Its goals are to improve job opportunities for these people, provide needed community services, rehabilitate participants, identify older people seeking employment, and generally improve their lives through training, job development, and placement.

To be eligible for the "Senior Aides" program, persons must be fifty-five or older, and have limited incomes. They must be certified eligibles by the State Employment Service and be covered by Social Security. Beyond that, benefits may include workmen's compensation, unemployment insurance and other fringe benefits. In addition, these "Aides" are granted an allowance for on-the-job aide-incurred expenses such as transportation to and from work or supplies needed in performing the job.

Additional information can be secured by contacting the U.S. Department of Labor, Washington, D.C. 20210.

WOMAN POWER

Job opportunities for women are on the increase. Some women make their family and home their career, while others combine the home with a second career. To the woman who wants to and can accept the responsibility of two careers, there are numerous opportunities waiting for you in the labor market.

Education, training, and professional preparation will enable you to develop yourself more fully, whether you marry or not, and will also make it easier for you to earn a living.

The untrained woman might consider going to school at a university, college, junior college, or business college to become professionally trained. Their curriculums are varied in order to give participants a choice for training. It might be well for you to survey the job market to determine where most opportunities lie before pursuing a course of study.

Employment patterns vary for different women. Some are able to work part-time while their children are in school, and others are able to work full-time. Working women should establish objectives and work toward a given end which will bring them maximum satisfaction. This could be in the form of monetary rewards or intrinsic satisfaction.

There are many new areas opening up to women in the fields of real estate, teaching, advertising, writing, painting, merchandising, interior decorating, or government work at either federal, state, or local levels. As these fields change and expand, they provide many opportunities for working women.

A woman with initiative, drive and determination can advance in the field she enters, because there is no one person that has a monopoly on all of the good ideas. The feminine mind can often open doors that have been previously closed to men.

Some women have aspired to become medical doctors, Congresswomen, Treasurers of the United States, generals in the Armed Forces, presidents of colleges, and in some foreign countries they hold positions equivalent to the President of the United States, and/or the Queen of their country.

In recent years, more than half of all women in the forty-five to fifty-four age group were either employed or looking for work and the same held true for forty percent of the women in the fifty-five to sixty-four age group.

There are many reasons why women must find full equality in the employment ranks; however, the best reason is they really need to work. There are well over one and one-half million women who have been abandoned by their husbands while more than two and one-half million women are widows. There are more than two million women who have been divorced and six million women are single. These women constitute upwards of forty percent of this nation's labor force.

More than twenty percent of the wives in America are working to help bring the family income above the poverty level.

In November of 1967, the United States Civil Service Commission established the Federal Women's Program under executive order 11375. Federal agencies were encouraged to bring more qualified women into the middle- and senior-level positions and greater emphasis was placed on the training these women received.

In 1969 the issuance of executive order 11478 resulted in nondiscrimination due to sex. Thus each department and agency of the federal government was obligated to "establish and maintain an affirmative program of equal employment opportunity for all civilian employees and applicants holding qualified credentials."

Research has indicated that older women workers have a number of good qualities to sell a potential employer:

1. Generally, turnover rates are smaller among older workers.

2. Attendance records on the job are better than younger workers.

3. Greater stability and concentration will usually permit the older worker to be more productive than the younger person.

4. Good working habits often have resulted from homemaking or volunteer work or from an earlier work experience.

5. Babysitting is no longer a problem.

There are some important things for you to consider before seeking a job. First, you must be sure you really want to work and second, the family must approve, otherwise the job will be a real burden to all concerned.

There is worth in every person. Each one can make a contribution to society in some field of endeavor, whether it be as a homemaker or a career woman in a professional area. The world of work awaits the challenging woman.

In the August 2, 1971, issue of *U. S. News & World Report,* the First Lady on Community Service indicates that "CARING FOR OTHERS CREATES THE SPIRIT OF A NATION." With this indomitable spirit, women will play a big part in the shaping of the future of the world. *There is no limit as to what women can do.*

Legal actions are continually eliminating restrictions which have limited women's employment possibilities. Some examples follow herewith.

An arbitrator ruled in 1970 that pantsuits are acceptable clothing for women teachers in the public schools of Kingsley, Michigan. The arbitrator said women lawyers in Michigan were wearing pantsuits before the Supreme Court, and that teachers had the same right to wear them.

———o———

A Wisconsin motel owner was ordered by the State's Department of Industry, Labor and Human Relations to offer a woman the job as manager after her initial application was turned down because she might "have to enter the room of a male occupant."

———o———

In Pennsylvania, a supermarket chain and a college were ordered by the U.S. District Court, under the Federal Equal Pay Act, to pay back wages to women who were doing jobs similar to men, who were, in some cases, making $1,000 a year more than the women.

TURN HOBBIES INTO DOLLARS

Hobbies acquired during working years can prove invaluable once you retire. First they will provide a meaningful way to spend idle hours and second, many people turn hobbies into supplemental income. Developing a hobby or hobbies early in life is important.

Many people at the turn of the century could not afford the luxury of a hobby because they had to work long, hard hours to make a living for their families. With more leisure time, today people have opportunities to do something besides work for a living.

Many older people became skilled in particular lines of work earlier in life. Some were self-taught and others learned craftsmanship from their fathers and forefathers. These skills, properly applied, can help people maintain more purchasing power, in addition to keeping themselves occupied.

AGE DISCRIMINATION IN EMPLOYMENT

Public Law 90–202, passed December 15, 1967, during the 90th Congress, makes it unlawful for an employer to fail or refuse to hire or to discharge (fire) any individual or otherwise discriminate against any individual with respect to his compensation, terms, conditions, or privileges of employment, because of such individual's age.

To get the pamphlet specifically dealing with job discrimination because of age, write your congressman in either the United States Senate or House of Representatives and ask him to secure pamphlet 81–Stat.–602 pertaining to the Age Discrimination Act for you.

EQUAL EMPLOYMENT OPPORTUNITY IS THE LAW
DISCRIMINATION IS PROHIBITED

Title VII of the Civil Rights Act of 1964, Administered by THE EQUAL EMPLOYMENT OPPORTUNITY COMMISSION, prohibits discrimination because of RACE, COLOR, RELIGION, SEX or NATIONAL ORIGIN by EMPLOYERS with 75 or more employees, by LABOR ORGANIZATIONS with a hiring hall or 75 or more members, by EMPLOYMENT AGENCIES, and by JOINT LABOR-MANAGEMENT COMMITTEES FOR APPRENTICESHIP OR TRAINING. After July 1, 1967, employers and labor organizations with 50 or more employees or members will be covered; after July 1, 1968, those with 25 or more will be covered. ANY PERSON who believes he or she has been discriminated against SHOULD CONTACT

THE EQUAL EMPLOYMENT
OPPORTUNITY COMMISSION
1800 G Street N.W.
Washington, D.C. 20506

Executive Order Number 11246, administered by THE OFFICE OF FEDERAL CONTRACT COMPLIANCE, prohibits discrimination because of RACE, COLOR, CREED or NATIONAL ORIGIN, and requires affirmative action to ensure equality of opportunity in all aspects of employment by all FEDERAL GOVERNMENT CONTRACTORS AND SUBCONTRACTORS, and by CONTRACTORS PERFORMING WORK UNDER A FEDERALLY ASSISTED CONSTRUCTION CONTRACT, regardless of the number of employees in either case.

ANY PERSON who believes he or she has been discriminated against SHOULD CONTACT

THE OFFICE OF FEDERAL
CONTRACT COMPLIANCE
U.S. Department of Labor
Washington, D.C. 20210

SEX DISCRIMINATION LAW

The Federal Civil Rights Act, Title VII–State Fair Employment Practices Laws–Executive Orders is listed in the 1964 Federal Civil Rights Act.

This particular act spells out job discrimination against women. The Woman's Bureau of the Wage and Labor Standards Administration of the U.S. Department of Labor can provide pamphlets with all of the detailed information on job discrimination because of sex.

PRIVATE EMPLOYMENT AGENCIES

Private employment agencies will be a good source for jobs because many of them specialize in specific areas, while counseling firms generally do only testing and counseling and do not help one find jobs. Before signing a contract with one of these firms, know *exactly* what they will do for you. If you are in doubt about one of these companies or a firm that you contemplate going to work for, consult the local Better Business Bureau for advice. Fees vary considerably from one organization to another. Be familiar with fees and payment schedules.

A reputable agency will be concerned with a worker's future and career and will really extend itself to assist you in finding a job.

7

Credentials--Letters--The Resume

ALL THAT YOU ARE, KNOW, REPRESENT, AND WOULD LIKE TO BE, must be projected when you present yourself orally and in writing to a prospective employer.

This chapter gives you guidelines and an opportunity to prepare written descriptions and express your desires for securing a job. Be accurate, brief, concise, follow proper protocol, and prepare each document carefully, as if your life depended on it. It can mean the difference between your getting and not getting a job.

CREDENTIALS AND RECORDS

A set of credentials is composed of individual records, transcripts, references, and student teaching and/or experience ratings, all of which should have a fairly recent date. In preparing credentials it is best to fill out the forms with a typewriter whose keys are clean, and the form should be free from errors or strikeovers. If this is not possible, be sure your handwriting is legible. Too often if you fill out the forms by hand, the person reading your credentials cannot read your handwriting. References contained in your file should be of recent date. If you are finishing a degree soon, list current courses you are taking.

Once you have registered with the placement service, all credentials become confidential and are the property of that organization. At no time will any of these confidential documents be revealed to you, unless it is the forms that you filled out. Periodically the placement service requests that you bring your file up-to-date. The master set of credentials is not permitted to leave the office. When credentials are mailed to a prospective employer, copies of the master set are mailed.

Credentials should be prepared and mailed to the school district or company designated by the placement service. They will be mailed upon your request or upon the request of a prospective employer. Other mailings may be made upon the request of a faculty member, the initiative of the placement service, or on the request of another placement service. In most cases, credentials will be mailed only to a prospective employer. Each placement service has its own rules.

Credentials are kept up-to-date by the placement service. In doing so, it is important that immediate action be taken to submit changes in status as they occur. This will prevent a great influx of changes showing up during the peak of the recruiting season.

When there is a change in jobs or address or telephone number, the service should be notified immediately and a carbon copy of the letter should go to the alumni office to update its records.

LETTERS OF RECOMMENDATION

Letters of recommendation which become part of your credentials are among the most important and confidential documents in your placement file.

Recommendations should be solicited only from reputable persons that you know well. It is very important that you use references that are related to your work experience, rather than those with whom you are merely acquainted socially. These recommendations should come from responsible persons such as professors, supervisors, former employers, bankers, lawyers, doctors, businessmen, or someone who is familiar with your ability and capabilities. It is best *not* to use a relative as a reference. Recommendatory letters become a permanent part of your credentials. Poor recommendations can be very detrimental to you in seeking a job now or later in life.

A recommendation can be good, bad, indifferent, or somewhere in between. You should want nothing but good recommendations in your file.

In securing recommendations, always ask a person first to see if you can use his name as a reference. If you are certain that you can list a name as a reference, it is good business to let this person know you have done so, and tell him what type of job you are applying for. This will aid him as he prepares your recommendation. It will help him to know what to stress about you. If you are not certain whether or not an individual will give you a good recommendation, you should ask, *"May I assume that you will give me a good recommendation?"* If he says "Yes" then you will have to trust him. If he says "No," then do not list him as a reference.

Where recommendations are a part of your college placement file, they will be forwarded with your credentials when requested. This is the easiest and most practical manner in which to get recommendations in the hands of an interviewer. While you might occasionally ask individuals to send a letter of recommendation to one prospective employer, it might be overdoing a good thing if you ask him to send letters to numerous employers. Then too, some people that you list as a reference will not care to share with you their letters of recommendation. This fact alone emphasizes the importance of having letters of recommendation on file with your credentials.

What is a recommendation worth? Perhaps not more than the paper it is written on; however, it can be a valuable asset to you when job hunting, providing it is factual and convinces the reader that you have abilities that the employer is looking for. Anyone can get someone to say something good about him. So, again, what is a recommendation worth?

In compiling your credentials, the placement service will normally furnish you with reference forms for you to send to the people you have listed as a reference. In sending out this form be sure to ask the individual to list his title along with his name. Mention that you are enclosing a stamped, self-addressed envelope which is to be returned to the placement service. Thank the person for giving you the recommendation and tell him how much you appreciate this service.

When asking for a recommendation, if the placement service form is not available, ask the person giving the recommendation to use business stationery letterheads if possible, along with his title. Again, enclose a stamped, self-addressed envelope.

THE LETTER OF INQUIRY

If you want to make an inquiry about a possible vacancy, write a letter to the potential employer and state that you are inquiring whether or not a vacancy is going to occur. When writing this letter, abide by the principles of good letter writing. Use the sample letter of inquiry in this chapter as a guide. Be as careful in writing this letter as you would in writing a letter of application. Emphasize that it is a letter of inquiry, because it may be construed to be a letter of application.

Remember, this is only a piece of paper with writing on it; however, it does represent you and if a good impression is to be made, the work you send out must be perfect. Use good quality white stationery of standard 8½ x 11 inches in size.

THE LETTER OF APPLICATION

Once again, good quality standard size stationery should be used and preferably the letter should be typewritten. It is suggested that you use the sample letter of application in this chapter for form.

In preparing your letter, draft it first in longhand. After you make necessary corrections redraft it again and again until it is perfect. When this has been done, type it for the first time and be careful with all margins and spacing. Proofread your letter. If necessary, use the expertise of someone more adept than yourself to check for correct spelling, proper English usage and other possible errors, until you have the ability to complete a job like this yourself. After final approval, the letter should be typed perfectly in final form so as to be free from all errors. When completed, sign your name in longhand. Legally, *printing your name for a signature is not acceptable.* Use either blue or black ink.

If a letter must be written in longhand, write as legibly as possible. If your writing cannot be read, how much of a chance do you stand in getting a job? Be sure to produce a perfect letter each time you send out a letter of application. If you make a mistake, start over again and keep doing this until you produce a perfect copy. On your return address, it is best to print or type your name, address, and zip code.

Neat letters which are well written leave good impressions. Never mail a letter containing erasures, or one that was written with a typewriter with ink-filled keys, ink blots or other discolorations. Write on only one side of a sheet of paper and keep a carbon copy or Xerox copy of every letter mailed to an employer. Keeping a copy of each letter for future reference is very important. You should be able to get the entire contents of your letter on one side of a sheet of paper.

On all occasions, send original copies of letters of application. Carbon and Xerox copies will not do the job properly.

In your letter, state at the beginning the position for which you are applying and indicate where you learned about the vacancy. This permits making an association with the contact which has already been made for you.

Generally, it is not good practice to inquire or comment on the salary in your letter of application. Approximate salary schedules can be obtained from the placement service prior to submitting a letter of application.

If you contemplate changing jobs, check closely to make sure the change will be beneficial. In some cases people talk about changing jobs, only to find out they will not get a large enough salary increase to warrant a move. It generally takes a sizable raise to make a move worthwhile if the residence has to be changed and the family uprooted.

All letters of correspondence should be clear, concise yet complete, and as brief as possible. In many cases, the placement service will forward your credentials before you receive a notice of a vacancy. This helps you make more contacts and enhances your chances of landing a good job.

Note that the sample letters in this chapter were designed so that they cannot become stereotyped. A form letter does not allow for personal initiative, individuality, and creativity. Your letter should reflect you, because chances are this will be the first contact a prospective employer will have with you. You will want to greet and leave him with a favorable impression.

Bizarre or unusual approach type letters are only good when they land a job for you. *Be careful with this type of letter unless it really reflects you.*

PHOTO

The Equal Employment Opportunity Act prohibits employers from requesting a picture of you; however, if you want a prospective employer to see one of your pictures, then include a recent photo of yourself of good quality, prepared by a professional photographer, that is approximately 2½ x 3½ inches in size. Before sending out the photo, sign your name on the reverse side with the year the picture was taken. Write your name lightly with a pencil. The recipient of your photo may want to use it for publicity purposes. Pressing hard with a ball point pen may show through the picture, if and when it is reproduced. A photo with a slight smile is more readily accepted than one with a big toothy grin. The "big grin" may offend some employers. No matter how you slice the mustard, prospective employers are going to want to know what you look like. Some jobs require people of certain proportions and, therefore, a good photo will help the employer make up his mind whether you can fill his requirements or not. The decision is yours. If you send a photo, it probably should be enclosed with your letter of application and resume.

SAMPLE LETTER OF INQUIRY

Street Address
City, State, Zip Code
Date

Name
Title
Street Address
City, State, Zip Code

Dear Mr. Blank:

First paragraph — State that this is a letter of inquiry, name the position you are interested in, and ask whether or not a vacancy is anticipated.

Second paragraph — State when you will be graduated from college, the degree you will hold, from what institution, and your major and minor.

Third paragraph — Indicate your credentials are up-to-date, their location, and state you will be happy to forward them and submit your formal application if permitted to do so.

Fourth paragraph — Have an appropriate closing to help pave the way for an early reply by enclosing a stamped, self-addressed return envelope, by asking for an application blank if a vacancy exists, by giving your telephone number, or by offering some similar suggestion that will show appreciation for receiving a reply at his/her earliest convenience.

Very truly yours,

(Sign your name in blue or black ink)
Your Name (Typewritten)

Enclosure: (Use this method if you want to enclose material such as a resume or a photo.)

NOTE: The letter of inquiry can serve as a letter to introduce yourself to an employer and depending on the response, it could turn into a letter of application.

SAMPLE LETTER OF APPLICATION

Street Address
City, State, Zip Code
Date

Name
Title
Street Address
City, State, Zip Code

Dear Mr. Blank:

First paragraph — Explain why you are writing, indicate the position for which you are applying, and tell how you heard about the vacancy.

Second paragraph — Indicate why you are interested in working for this employer, and mention your interest in this type of work. If you have had experience related to the job you are applying for, list the specific achievements you accomplished in your field of work. State that you are interested in "a career" and not simply a paycheck for a few months or a year.

Third paragraph — Refer to the attached personal data sheet (resume) which gives a summary of your qualifications, your training, interests, and experience.

Fourth paragraph — Have an appropriate closing to help pave the way for the interview by enclosing a stamped, self-addressed return envelope, by giving your telephone number, or by making a suggestion that you will appreciate a reply at his/her convenience.

Very truly yours,

(Sign your name in blue or black ink)
Your Name (Typewritten)

Enclosure: (Use this method if you want to enclose material such as a resume or a photo.)

NOTE: If you are answering an advertisement from a newspaper, magazine or some other source, cover all points requested by the employer. This could be the way an employer tests your ability to follow instructions.

SAMPLE FOLLOW-UP LETTER

Street Address
City, State, Zip Code
Date

Name
Title
Street Address
City, State, Zip Code

Dear Mr. Blank:

First paragraph — Express appreciation for being granted the interview and the courtesies extended to you by the interviewer. Indicate the job for which you were interviewed, where the interview was conducted, and the date. Perhaps you will want to recall some pleasant incident that took place during the interview.

Second paragraph — Reaffirm your interest in the job or position for which you were interviewed. Briefly cover your reasons for wanting this type of work. If you have had relevant experiences since the interview that are of parallel interest, then give a short description of what occurred.

Third paragraph — Be willing to provide additional data which will clarify or strengthen your application. Hopefully all of this was covered, but in case it was not, make sure you cooperate with the employer.

Fourth paragraph — Indicate you are still interested in the position and that if other officials wish to interview you also, that you will be available at their convenience. Remember, be politely persistent while seeking that job.

Very truly yours,

(Sign your name in blue or black ink)
Your Name (Typewritten)

OTHER TYPES OF LETTERS

Persons seeking employment oftentimes find it necessary to write many types of letters. Some will be relative to an invitation to visit a particular employer, others will be in response to inquiries for information, and still others will be in the nature of follow-up actions resulting from your interview.

If you expect to be treated fairly by an employer, then you should expect to treat him fairly and with prompt action and this means answering each letter, telegram or telephone call promptly. A prompt reply will indicate you have initiative, determination, and a desire to succeed.

Primarily, the types of letters you will be most interested in — aside from the ones mentioned on previous pages — include the "stall letter," "letters of rejection," and "letters of acceptance."

STALL LETTERS

This type of letter is written to postpone any definite action and it is considered as an interim letter toward keeping the prospective position open for your consideration and possible acceptance.

In the first paragraph, refer to any preceding action calling for this particular letter, such as an offer, telegram, telephone call, letter, or anything else that indicates an interest in your services.

State that you are definitely interested in the position, but would like additional time (state how much) to reach a decision. Do not take too much time, because the employer may think you are putting him off unnecessarily and may decide to go ahead and hire someone else. If you would like additional information on several questions or items, state so and be specific. If there are other reasons why you cannot accept a position immediately state them and indicate when you can accept the job.

REJECTION LETTERS

These letters are written once you definitely decide to decline an offer of employment. It is an act of courtesy and good business to notify a prospective employer that you have arrived at this decision, because you may later ask this same employer for a job and past considerations on your part may weigh heavily either for or against you. This type of action shows you have concern for others.

This type of letter should start off with an appreciation for the offer and state that at this time you must turn it down. Repeat the details of the position which you applied for in order to make it easier for the employer to recall the position being discussed. Perhaps many other people applied for the same job. Briefly and concisely give a reason for rejecting the offer.

ACCEPTANCE LETTERS

This is the letter you have been waiting to write so compose it carefully. Be as meticulous as you were in the interview and in preparing other correspondence. Even though you are elated and happy and want to display some emotion about getting a job, proceed cautiously.

Write as soon as you decide to accept the offer. If a contract is to be signed, keep your copy in a safe place — also keep the letter or telegram offering the job to you in a safe place. This is just good business. If an offer is made over the telephone, ask that a letter be sent to you to confirm the offer.

Remember that this type of letter constitutes an employment contract (offer, acceptance, and other considerations are all involved). Do not write with the idea you can reject this job if a better opportunity comes along. The contents of your letter should include the exact details of your agreement: job title, place of employment, starting salary, number of hours to be worked each week, if applicable, in addition to any other relevant information.

Make sure that your pay is for a certain number of hours and how overtime, if any, is to be paid. Some companies do not have overtime and give compensatory time off in lieu of pay. Check the local policy regarding this matter.

Indicate the time you can report for work. If the employer

asks for a specific date for you to begin work, be in a position to relate your reasons if you prefer to wait. However, it is best to go out of your way to report at the time the employer wants your services. The more easily you can fit into a new position, the better it will be for you during the adjustment period.

State you are looking forward to working for the firm, company or school district and express appreciation for being given an opportunity to share your career with them. A positive statement will indicate you are willing to do a good job and will work hard to be successful.

THE RESUME

A resume is the summary of an individual applying for a job. It has been said the resume is the most important document the average person will ever write, and literally it should be a "picture" of you.

The resume is the document that helps secure the interview and because of this factor, it has become indispensable for the job hunter. The well-prepared resume will provide a valuable source of information for the person conducting the interview and it will, if prepared properly, reflect the type of person who is applying for employment.

Several forms of resumes are presented in this chapter and it is important for you to study them all and then select the format that is best suited to help you project yourself.

Ordinarily the resume should be short — between one and one and one-half pages. However, there may be some instances where a longer resume may be required. If your short resume is of sufficient interest to an employer, he may ask for more detailed information, and you should then be prepared to forward more precise material. There may be a few occasions where corporate executives or highly specialized individuals may need to prepare a more extensive resume. In most cases the short resume is preferable. The big three- and four-page resumes generally do not get the attention the short, well-prepared summaries do. When preparing a resume, pick out the most important things to present and know the employer well enough to anticipate what will be important to him. A blanket resume is fine and easily prepared; however, if you are applying to several firms, some of which may be different from others, it would be advisable to prepare a special resume to fit each letter of application. Keep a copy of all correspondence with each employer. Always tell the truth, state facts, then you will never have to worry about what you might have said during an interview or conversation about employment with a prospective employer.

RESUME CONTENTS

The job objective is probably the most important part of your resume. State as clearly and concisely as possible what type of job you are searching for. If a prospective employer can spot your potential and skills quickly, he will review your resume, especially if there is an opening in your area of interest.

The resume should be easy to read and pictorially easy to follow.

Personal information should include age, height, weight, marital status, children and their ages, health, hobbies, clubs, and if you own or rent a home or live with your parents, and if you are willing to relocate. Stating you are interested only in one or two geographic areas will limit employment opportunities.

Education is important and all degrees should be listed, the years granted, type of degree and name of institution. If a person is a college or university graduate, the high school record is usually not required. List major and minor areas of study as well as class standing, if known. Other useful items will include offices held, organizations belonged to, honors received, community participation, scholarships, grants, and whether or not you were employed. If you were, describe the type of work that you did and give your employer's name and address.

95

The General Resume

Your employment record should start with the current job, or most recent one, and work backwards, giving dates of employment and reasons for leaving. With each job, record the name of your supervisor (boss) and his address and telephone number. Prospective employers may want to contact some of your past employers.

Many applicants simply state "credentials" or "references sent on request." By using this method, if a prospective employer asks for credentials or references, this is an indication that he is interested in you.

From a corporate executive to an X-ray technician to a teacher, regardless of the section of the nation, the resume may be the key that opens the door of employment for you. Prepare it so the REAL YOU will be projected in a favorable image.

A good salesman has to be sold on the product he is selling. You must be sold on your abilities and future well enough to enable you to sit down and prepare your credentials in such a manner as to sell yourself.

It is best to prepare several rough drafts of the resume before typing it in final form. While you may make up a resume with a typewriter, it is best to get a professional printing job, such as an offset-printed resume on 8½ x 11 inches of good quality white bond paper. You should not use carbon copies or mimeograph copies of a resume to send to an employer. Photocopies of resumes are acceptable if they are neat, clean, and legible. A responsible printing firm can print your resume for a reasonable price.

People very seldom fall into an excellent job. Ordinarily they plan ahead, prepare themselves, and when the opportunity presents itself, they are ready to take advantage of it.

THE GENERAL RESUME

A general resume is the best pattern to follow for those having previous experience where they worked for a salary. Employment and placement agencies may be more effective in finding employment for the individual who uses this resume. It can also be used by those seeking a change in employment.

In the upper left-hand corner list your name, address, and telephone number. Under "Occupational Goal" indicate the type of job desired.

Under the heading "Education," it is permissible to omit the high school record if you attended or graduated from college, unless you attended a vocational-type high school and are applying for a job in conjunction with high school training and/or experience. Give main course of study and indicate the percentage of total hours earned in this specialty — i.e., forty hours in biology which comprised approximately one-third of total hours earned for a bachelor's degree. List any special schooling or courses taken, giving length of course, date of completion, as well as the agency which conducted the course — for example, General Motors, Zenith, or New York Life.

Under work experience, list the last three or four jobs held, placing them in reverse order. Some job applications may call for more, especially if the three or four jobs held cover less than a five-year span. Give the full name of the company, the position or title held, the immediate supervisor's name, address and telephone number, dates of employment, and the complete address of the company. With each job listed, give a brief description of your duties and responsibilities.

If you have not worked for awhile, it is important to list skills and indicate any equipment you are capable of operating.

Enumerate community activities, especially volunteer work, because most employers like to see their employees active in the local community. List name, address and telephone number of the agency served, person familiar with what you actually did, the type of work or service rendered and dates of service. This would include organizations such as Red Cross, March of Dimes, Community Chest, Cancer Society, Easter Seals, and Big Brothers.

Under personal data, list age. (Do not omit age unless a resume

The General Resume

is being prepared according to "40-Plus Club" resume instructions, where the employer can get an indication of your age by noting the years of experience in various fields of work or length of jobs held.) Marital status and number of dependents are important because many employers consider a family man to be more reliable, especially if he is past twenty-eight years of age.

If you have a special driver's license or any other occupational license or certificate to perform the job you are applying for, mention it.

RESUME

John Q. Doe   PERMANENT ADDRESS:
42 & Plowed Ground   445 Foreflusher Loop
Leonard, Texas 75425   Flagstaff, Arizona 86001
TELEPHONE: 817/222-1111   602/774-9232

AGE: 33   BIRTH DATE: July 8, 1939
HEIGHT: 6′ 1″   WEIGHT: 218

OCCUPATIONAL GOAL: To be the director of public relations for a firm, school district, college or university.

EDUCATION:

School and Location	Dates	Degree
Northern Ariz. Univ., Flagstaff, Arizona	1968–72	EdS
Major: Education Minor: Journalism		
Northern Ariz. Univ., Flagstaff, Arizona	1966–68	MA
Major: Administration Minor: English		
Univ. of Northern Colorado, Greeley, Colo.	1963–66	BA
Major: Education Minor: Journalism		
Trinidad JC, Trinidad, Colorado	1961–63	AA
Major: Education Minor: Journalism		

WORK EXPERIENCE:

Public Information Office, Northern Arizona University, 1966 to present; one summer (1963) with the *Arizona Daily Star*, Tucson,

Arizona; three years with the *Greeley Daily Tribune*, Greeley, Colorado (1963–66); two years with the *Chronicle News* (daily), Trinidad, Colorado (1961–3); freelance writing and photography as well as freelance public relations for six years; have had seventy-five stories and photographs accepted for national publication.

COLLEGE HONORS AND AWARDS:

Was named the top writer for the student newspaper at the University of Northern Colorado in 1964. Earned a scholastic scholarship from Trinidad Junior College to the University of Northern Colorado. While at Trinidad, I was named one of the top ten students that participated in the college band and wrote for the newspaper and yearbook, where I received national awards.

EXTRA-CURRICULAR ACTIVITIES:

Writer-photographer for student newspaper at the University of Northern Colorado. Writer-photographer for student newspaper and yearbook at Trinidad Junior College. Played football, wrestled and was member of the track team at Trinidad.

MILITARY EXPERIENCE:

Served in the United States Air Force from 1956–60 and received an honorable discharge. Was a B-47 crew chief and served in Hawaii, Guam, and in Japan.

PROFESSIONAL ORGANIZATIONS:

Sigma Delta Chi — International Journalism Society
Phi Delta Kappa — National Honorary Educational Fraternity
Kappa Delta Pi — Educational Society for Educators
(List student organizations such as clubs, societies, fraternities, etc.)

DATE AVAILABLE:

Will be available on or after November 1972.

REFERENCES:

Credentials and references sent upon request.

Functional Resume No. 1

CREDENTIAL LOCATION:

Credentials are located in the placement offices at the University of Northern Colorado and Northern Arizona University.

FUNCTIONAL RESUME NO. 1

This resume is the one most often used by seniors graduating from college who are seeking a job for the first time. In graphic form it represents YOU to an employer. This resume may be used for both on-campus and off-campus interviews; however, it is considered indispensable for off-campus interviews. If you should send a letter of application to a prospective employer, include a resume with the letter. When answering an advertisement regarding a job, a resume should be included. If job-hunting should be done on a "cold-canvas" basis, a resume should be included with your letter of application.

Your resume should be neat, orderly, comparatively brief, and without error or typewritten or handwritten strikeovers.

Recent college graduates will emphasize their educational background, extra-curricular activities, and part-time jobs which helped to defray their college expenses. If you are more experienced you will begin by stressing your past employment record, with less emphasis on things such as college activities.

The resume must indicate that you have those qualities being sought by the employer. If you are looking for a position in which you would have to deal with people, then you will need to emphasize extra-curricular activities and mention what you have done that demonstrated your leadership ability.

RESUME

John Q. Doe	PERMANENT ADDRESS:
102 Hackberry Lane	1109 Circle Lane
New York, New York 10017	Syracuse, New York 13202
TELEPHONE: 212/345-6789	315/632-1234
AGE: 22 BIRTH DATE: Nov. 5, 1950	

HEIGHT: 5' 10"   WEIGHT: 165

OCCUPATIONAL GOAL: To become a city planner or urban developer. Am willing to work toward a career and am not interested in making frequent moves for salary only, as I am looking for a long-range job.

EDUCATION:

School and Location	Dates	Degree
Syracuse University, Syracuse, N.Y.	1971–73	BS
Major: Urban Planning Minor: Math		
New York Trade Institute, Albany, N.Y.	1969–71	AS
Major: Planning Minor: Math		

WORK EXPERIENCE:

Part-time employee in City Planner's Office for City of Syracuse (1971–73). Responsible for helping chart all new growth areas. Worked more than 3,000 hours in two years while going to school.

While at the New York Trade Institute in Albany, I worked with the City Planner's Office on a part-time basis (1969–71). Helped in Urban Renewal and worked approximately 2,000 hours during this period.

COLLEGE HONORS AND AWARDS:

Was graduated from New York Trade Institute in Albany, 8th in a class of 251 and currently rank 47th in a senior class of 1,098 at Syracuse University. Have been named to the Dean's honor list all four years in college.

VOLUNTEER WORK:

Helped with the American Cancer Society's drives in Syracuse and Albany.

EXTRA-CURRICULAR ACTIVITIES:

Photography Club at New York Trade Institute. Debate teams at New York Institute and Syracuse University. Had two photographs and three stories accepted by *U. S. News & World Report* on Urban Development. Belonged to ROTC at Syracuse.

DATE AVAILABLE:
Immediately.

PERSONAL REFERENCES:
References will be provided upon request. (If references are a part of your placement service file, state that they will be sent with your credentials.)

Credentials are located at Syracuse University's Placement Service.

FUNCTIONAL RESUME NO. 2

Functional Resume No. 2 is especially designed to fit the needs of the mature woman who is seeking work and has little or no employment record, has been strictly a volunteer worker, or has not worked for a number of years.

This type of resume puts the spotlight on volunteer services and activities as well as the educational background and these things are of prime importance for the employer selecting someone who has limited work experience.

Also, this type of resume proves beneficial if a person has a variety of skills or experiences that may require a person to make frequent changes in job assignments. A flexible person can generally find employment more quickly, especially if the employer is aware of her ability to function well in several capacities.

In preparing this resume, focus on the kind of work you are looking for, describing the job you want to do instead of mentioning a specific job title. By being descriptive, the employer will know that you know what you are talking about.

For women returning to work or seeking work for the first time after several years from time of graduation, state the family arrangements needed, such as a baby-sitter, the family's approval, and any other relevant information. List any unusual circumstances that might need explanation. It is better to explain a situation than have a prospective employer assume something that is not true.

This also applies to women entering the labor force late in life or reentering after a delay of some kind — a woman who has raised a family and now wants to go back to work or a woman needing work because of illness of the husband or being widowed or divorced.

RESUME

Jane Z. Doe   PERMANENT ADDRESS:
2730 North Fremont Boulevard   2730 North Fremont Blvd.
Bakersfield, California 93309   Bakersfield, California 93309
TELEPHONE: 805/321-9876   805/321-9876

AGE: 33   BIRTH DATE: August 8, 1940

HEIGHT: 5′ 6″   WEIGHT: 127

OCCUPATIONAL GOAL: To become involved in a nursing program to the extent where I can make a significant contribution to the profession. Am willing to take advanced courses as directed.

EDUCATION:

School and Location	Dates	Degree
Bakersfield JC, Bakersfield, Calif.	1964–65	None
Major: Nursing Minor: Biology		
Fresno State College, Fresno, Calif.	1965–68	BS; RN
Major: Nursing Minor: Nutrition		
University of Southern California, Los Angeles, Calif.		
Major: Nursing Minor: Administration	1968–70	MS

WORK EXPERIENCE:

From 1970 until present, I have been employed at the Memorial Hospital in Bakersfield; however, due to my husband being trans-

103

ferred to San Diego, I will be forced to leave my current position on July 1. Worked as RN and shift supervisor.

VOLUNTEER WORK:
   Have been involved in Scouting for the last eight years. Helped with United Fund Drives the last four years and worked with the Red Cross for two years.

ORGANIZATIONS:
   Junior Women's Club in Bakersfield
   Homemakers Club

DATE AVAILABLE:
   Family will start moving to San Diego about July 1 and will take about a month to get settled. Will be available on August 1. If an emergency should occur, I could be available on July 15.

PERSONAL REFERENCES:
   References will be provided upon request. (If references are a part of your placement service file, state they will be sent with your credentials.)
   Credentials are located at the Placement Service, University of Southern California. (If credentials are not on file or if you have none, say so; however, you can still have letters of recommendation sent or provide references as requested.)

FUNCTIONAL RESUME NO. 3

This resume is designed specifically for the job-seeker who has no college training and wants to enter the job market directly out of high school.

   Since education is limited to high school and special sessions with organizations that do not offer a degree, other than the high school diploma, references are of prime importance because it is these references that must spell out your ability and potential. The references must also point out your willingness to learn new things, how well you work with other individuals, and how you accept and implement suggestions from the "boss."

An occupational goal is also important because if you point out a strong desire to learn something that will be of benefit to you as well as to the company from whom you are seeking a job, that company will look at you carefully and with greater interest.

Honors, awards, hobbies and interest areas are more important for the non-college graduate because these help a potential employer "weigh" the individual.

Many good jobs can be held with a high school diploma if you are willing to attend special training sessions once you are on the job.

More persistence will be needed and you will have to be capable of laying your potential on the line because you will not have the college placement service to do this for you. State employment agencies can be a prime source of help.

RESUME

John Q. Doe
321 E. Crammer
Harlan, Kansas 64422
TELEPHONE: 341/241-1457

PERMANENT ADDRESS:
123 Solomon Avenue
Portis, Kansas 64321
340/219-1293

AGE: 18   BIRTH DATE: January 1, 1955

HEIGHT: 6' 2"   WEIGHT: 195

OCCUPATIONAL GOAL: To secure a job where there is advancement opportunity to lay a solid foundation for a career. In high school I had three years of vocational education and two years of distributive education.

EDUCATION:

School and Location	Dates	Degree
Portis High, Portis, Kansas	1970–71	Diploma

Functional Resume No. 3

Portis High   1967–70   Diploma
Summer Distributive Education program at Portis High in 1971.
  Area of Study
Vocational Education
College Preparatory

WORK EXPERIENCE:

Worked after school and on Saturdays in a produce house, service station, and in a grocery store and meat market. Three summers were spent working in the harvest fields. During my senior year I worked on Saturdays in the Lee Supermarket. Was required to handle advertising and grocery displays.

HONORS AND AWARDS:

Was named the top Distributive Education student in 1971. Advertising and marketing project was judged the best in the school, as judged by the Portis Chamber of Commerce, for the 1970–71 school year. Senior year was captain of the basketball team; a member of the boys' octette; President of the Senior Class; President of Student Council; and carried a lead in the Senior play.

VOLUNTEER WORK:

Was an assistant in the local Boy Scout program during my junior and senior years in high school.

HOBBIES:

Stamp collecting, coin collecting, hunting and fishing.

DATE AVAILABLE:

July 1, 1973

REFERENCES:

G. W. Caldwell, Director, Board of Education, 100 Nichols Dr., Harlan, Kansas 64422

J. E. Kissell, Editor, Portis Independent, 19 Thomas St., Portis, Kansas 64411

W. E. Lee, Editor, Smith County Pioneer, 124 Windscheffel Ave., Smith Center, Kansas 65226

Charles Lee, Manager, Lee's Supermarket, 321 Turner Crt., Portis, Kansas 64411

Lewis Naylor, Superintendent of Schools, 69 Wolters St., Portis, Kansas 64411

John Anderson, Treasurer, Board of Education, Box 321, RR 1, Harlan, Kansas 64422

FUNCTIONAL RESUME NO. 4

An offset printed resume of this type, made up with the photograph printed in the upper right hand corner of the front page, illustrates how you may include your picture in this style of a vita. A quality application size photo, taken by a professional photographer, should be used. From this the printer can make a halftone picture and print it on the resume sheet.

While the format of this particular resume is slightly different than those listed previously, it demonstrates another pattern or approach that can be used, depending on your personal preference. Adjustments or positioning of sub-head sections can be made according to choice, as long as it does not violate a conventional format that is recognized by authorities in the field. It still permits you to be brief, concise, yet complete, with clarity. By radiating quality in preparing the resume, it indicates to the prospective employer the standards, image and portrayal you want to depict and represent.

When preparing and producing this type of a resume, here are some of the advantages and disadvantages you may encounter:

ADVANTAGES

1. Personalizes resume.
2. Identifies your face with the application.
3. If you are photogenic it will be to your advantage — it will depend on to whom you are applying and for what purpose.

4. Represents quality of effort and that "extra mile" you are willing to go in presenting and selling yourself when seeking a job.
5. A little additional expense that helps you get a job may be returned "tenfold."

DISADVANTAGES

1. A prospective employer may make a premature subjective judgment that could be detrimental to an applicant. It is possible the employer may not judge you on your true merits and ability as indicated in the resume and letter of application.
2. Increases cost of production.
3. If you are not photogenic it could be to your disadvantage — again, it will depend on to whom you are applying and for what purpose.
4. A minor deterrent could occur when the recipient of the resume does not have a separate photo to use for newspaper release purposes, if and when required; however, one can always be forwarded later if needed.

The sample resume can be used in two parts or as one entity. The first page contains essential information and the second one lists "nice to know" data. Most employers will want to see the complete resume, *which should not run over two pages.* It is preferable to limit the entire resume contents to one page when possible.

Even though this type of resume is preferred by many people, you may encounter a situation where the prospective employer may submit his own version of a standardized resume outline and request you to follow his directions in filling it out.

By adopting the philosophy that "it only costs a little more to go first class," it can be of immeasurable value to you. This needs to be tempered with the type of judgment that permits you to know when and where to strike a "happy medium" in your selection process.

RESUME

NAME
James Otto Berg, Ed.D.

HOME ADDRESS
1600 E. Hillside Dr. Apt. 35
Bloomington, Indiana 47401
812/332-8214

BUSINESS ADDRESS
School of HPER
Indiana University
Bloomington, Indiana 47401
812/337-1604

PERSONAL DATA
Date of Birth: July 6, 1935
Height 5' 11", Weight 180
Married, 2 children
Health: excellent
Hometown: Jamestown, Kansas

EDUCATION

B.S.   1958   Kansas State University, Manhattan, Kansas
                Major: Physical Education
                Minor: Science and Health

M.Ed.   1963   University of Arizona, Tucson, Arizona
                Major: Physical Education
                Minor: Education and Health

Ed.D.   1969   University of Missouri, Columbia, Missouri
                Major: Higher Education Administration and
                       Physical Education
                Minor: Measurement and Research

EXPERIENCE

1959–61 San Diego City Schools, San Diego, California
         Outdoor Education Teacher

1961–62   Wheeler Public Schools, Wheeler, Indiana
          8th Grade Teacher (all subjects), Jr. High Principal
          and Athletic Coach

1962–63   University of Arizona, Tucson, Arizona
          Freshmen Baseball Coach (while working on M.Ed.
          degree)

1963–65   University of Arizona, Tucson, Arizona
          Director of Educational Placement and Head Resident
          of a Men's Residence Hall

1965–66   University of Iowa, Iowa City, Iowa
          Graduate Assistant in Physical Education (while doing
          graduate work)

1966–67   University of Missouri, Columbia, Missouri
          Instructor in Physical Education (while working on
          Ed.D. degree)

1967–69   University of Iowa, Iowa City, Iowa
          Director of Intramural and Recreational Sports

1969–   Indiana University, Bloomington, Indiana
          Director of Intramural Sports and Assistant Professor
          of Physical Education

RESUME
James Otto Berg
page 2

RECENT PUBLICATIONS

"Recreational Facilities and Equipment," *Campus Recreation,*
American Association for Health, Physical Education and Recreation, Washington, D.C., NEA Publications, Washington, D.C.,
1968.

"Future Trends in the Administration of Intramural Sports at the
Collegiate Level," *20th Annual Proceedings of the National Intramural Association,* November, 1969.

"Differences Between Male Participants and Non-participants in a College IM Sports Program in Regard to Academic Achievement and Academic Ability," *21st Annual Proceedings of the National Intramural Association*, September, 1970.

PROFESSIONAL AFFILIATIONS

Phi Delta Kappa

Phi Epsilon Kappa

American Educational Research Association

American Association for Health, Physical Education and Recreation

National College Physical Education Association for Men

NTL Institute for Applied Behavioral Science

National Intramural Association

National Intramural Sports Council

Big Ten Intramural Sports Directors Association

Past member of ASCUS, Rocky Mountain College Placement Association and Western College Placement Association

HONORS AND AWARDS

Recipient of the Phi Epsilon Kappa National Efficiency Achievement Award in 1958

A principal speaker at the National Conference on College and University Recreation held in Washington, D.C., 1968

Received a monetary research grant from the NIA in 1968 and 1969

Member of the National Touch Football Rules Committee 1968 to present

State Representative in Iowa for the NISC 1968-69

Chairman of the Big Ten Intramural Sports Directors Association 1969–70

Appointed to the NIA national nominating committee 1970–71

Functional Resume No. 4

Introduced the Keynote Speaker at the NIA national convention in 1971

Member of the NIA resolutions committee 1971–72

GENERAL INFORMATION

Leisure Interests — Paddleball, golf, hunting, fishing, jogging, meeting people, reading, public speaking and travel

Community Activities — Civic Newcomers Club, Toastmasters Club

Other Experiences — U.S. Marine Corps Veteran, four year athletic scholarship and baseball letterman at Kansas State, forest fire fighter in Alaska, canoe trip leader in Canada and Wisconsin, semi-pro baseball player in Kansas and Nebraska, Kappa Sigma social fraternity

APPENDIX I

QUESTIONS FREQUENTLY ASKED DURING THE EMPLOYMENT INTERVIEW

*as reported by 92 companies surveyed by Frank S. Endicott,
former Director of Placement, Northwestern University*

1. What are your future vocational plans?
2. In what school activities have you participated? Why? Which did you enjoy the most?
3. How do you spend your spare time? What are your hobbies?
4. In what type of position are you most interested?
5. Why do you think you might like to work for our company?
6. What jobs have you held? How were they obtained and why did you leave?
7. What courses did you like best? Least? Why?
8. Why did you choose your particular field of work?
9. What percentage of your college expenses did you earn? How?
10. How did you spend your vacations while in school?
11. What do you know about our company?
12. Do you feel that you have received a good general training?
13. What qualifications do you have that make you feel that you will be successful in your field?
14. What extracurricular offices have you held?
15. What are your ideas on salary?
16. How do you feel about your family?
17. How interested are you in sports?
18. If you were starting college all over again, what courses would you take?
19. Can you forget your education and start from scratch?
20. Do you prefer any specific geographic location? Why?

21. Do you have marriage plans?
22. How much money do you hope to earn at age 30? 35?
23. Why did you decide to go to this particular school?
24. How did you rank in your graduating class in high school? Where will you probably rank in college?
25. Do you think that your extracurricular activities were worth the time you devoted to them? Why?
26. What do you think determines one's progress in a good company?
27. What personal characteristics are necessary for success in your chosen field?
28. Why do you think you would like this particular type of job?
29. What is your father's occupation?
30. Tell me about your home life during the time you were growing up.
31. Are you looking for a permanent or temporary job?
32. Do you prefer working with others or by yourself?
33. Who are your best friends?
34. What kind of boss do you prefer?
35. Are you primarily interested in making money or do you feel that service to your fellow man is a satisfactory accomplishment?
36. Can you take instructions without feeling upset?
37. Tell me about the best book you have read recently.
38. Do you live with your parents? Which of your parents has had the most profound influence on you?
39. How did previous employers treat you?
40. What have you learned from some of the jobs you have had?
41. Can you get recommendations from previous employers?
42. What interests you about our product or service?
43. Have you had any kind of military training?
44. Have you ever changed your major field of interest while in college? Why?
45. When did you choose your college major?
46. How do your college grades compare with those you earned in high school?
47. Do you feel you have done the best scholastic work of which you are capable?
48. How did you happen to go to college?
49. What do you know about opportunities in the field in which you are trained?
50. How long do you expect to work?

51. Have you ever had any difficulty getting along with fellow students and faculty?
52. Which of your college years was the most difficult?
53. What is the source of your spending money?
54. Do you own any life insurance?
55. Have you saved any money?
56. Do you have any debts?
57. How old were you when you began to earn money?
58. Do you like to attend concerts?
59. Did you enjoy your four years at this university?
60. Do you like routine work?
61. Do you like regular hours?
62. What size city do you prefer?
63. Have you ever contributed to the family income?
64. What is your major weakness?
65. Define cooperation!
66. Will you struggle to get ahead?
67. Do you demand attention?
68. Do you have an analytical mind?
69. Are you eager to please?
70. What do you do to keep in good physical condition?
71. How do you usually spend vacations?
72. Have you had any serious illness or injury?
73. Are you willing to go where the company sends you?
74. What job in our company would you choose if you were entirely free to do so?
75. Is it an effort for you to be tolerant of persons with a background and interests different from your own?
76. What types of books have you read?
77. Have you plans for graduate work?
78. What types of people seem to "rub you the wrong way"?
79. Do you enjoy sports as a participant? As an observer?
80. Have you ever tutored an underclassman?
81. What jobs have you enjoyed the most? The least? Why?
82. What are your own special abilities?
83. What job in our company do you want to work toward?
84. Would you prefer a large or a small company? Why?
85. What is your idea of how industry operates today?
86. Do you like to travel?

87. How about overtime work?
88. What kind of work interests you?
89. What are the disadvantages of your chosen field?
90. Do you think that grades should be considered by employers? Why or why not?
91. Are you interested in research?
92. If married, how often do you entertain at home?
93. What is your opinion of the use of liquor?
94. What have you done which shows initiative and willingness to work?

APPENDIX II

1. Someone who has the ability to get along with other people.
2. Someone who is not afraid to work.
3. Someone who is not a clock watcher.
4. Someone who does not want 10 minutes off for 5 minutes overtime.
5. Someone who is faithful and loyal to the employer.
6. Someone who can follow as well as lead.
7. Someone who is reliable and dependable.
8. Someone who has initiative.
9. Someone who has a desire to get ahead.
10. Someone who is gregarious — an extrovert.
11. Someone who follows the golden rule.
12. Someone who is honest and possesses integrity.
13. Someone whose character is above reproach.
14. Someone who is willing to go to the job instead of having the job come to him.
15. Someone who knows how to dress to fit the occasion.
16. Someone who knows how to use "common horse sense."
17. Someone who will sacrifice personally for the firm when the occasion demands.
18. Someone who knows how to control his temper.
19. Someone who has a pleasing personality.
20. Someone who has poise and good bearing when under chaotic circumstances.
21. Someone who is well-read and capable of talking on different levels about varied subjects.
22. Someone who knows how to be firm, yet fair, just and honest.

23. Someone who knows how to establish good rapport with others.
24. Someone who follows a good code of ethics.
25. Someone who is looking for a permanent job.
26. Someone who is tolerant of others.
27. Someone having a career objective.
28. Someone who desires to progress and is willing to change with the times.
29. Someone who keeps good eye contact when talking to you.
30. Someone who is polite, courteous, tactful and diplomatic.
31. Someone who is mature.
32. Someone who has a sense of humor.
33. Someone who knows how to delegate and/or accept both responsibility and authority.
34. Someone who has an interest in community activities.
35. Someone who knows how to ask intelligent questions about a firm.
36. Someone who can take constructive criticism.
37. Someone who has good credit and is capable of taking care of his personal finances.
38. Someone who is capable of adjusting himself to the level of of the person he is talking to, without lowering himself.
39. Someone who possesses "social graces."
40. Someone who has foresight and does not have "tunnel vision."
41. Someone who is energetic, prompt and efficient.
42. Someone who can make policy and decisions.
43. Someone who has the ability to communicate effectively.
44. Someone willing to start at the bottom and work up.
45. Someone who is not a job-jumper.
46. Someone who feels, "There 'Ain't Nothing' we can't do."
47. Someone who can adapt himself to a community or a situation.
48. Someone who is confident in his ability.
49. Someone who is temperate in his habits.
50. Someone who gets an idea a minute and can't wait to get started on tomorrow.
51. Someone who works smarter, not harder.
52. Someone who believes that whatever the mind of man can conceive and believe, it can achieve.
53. Someone who realizes he cannot get much done in life if he just works on days when he feels good.
54. Someone who understands the effort and dedication needed to be good at his job.

55. Someone who realizes if he is satisfied he is "dead."
56. Someone who knows how to hold a job after he gets it.
57. Someone who has faith in himself and his inner strengths.
58. Someone who realizes life is not a utopia.
59. Someone who realizes that people who need people are the luckiest people in the world.
60. Someone who realizes he is as good as the best thing he ever did.
61. Someone who realizes it takes only one idea, followed by action, to succeed when others fail.
62. Someone who realizes that luck is the residue of design.
63. Someone who plans for the future for he may want to spend the rest of his life there.

APPENDIX III

NEGATIVE FACTORS EVALUATED DURING THE EMPLOYMENT INTERVIEW
AND WHICH FREQUENTLY LEAD TO REJECTION OF THE APPLICANT

*as reported by 153 companies surveyed by Frank S. Endicott,
former Director of Placement, Northwestern University*

1. Poor personal appearance.
2. Overbearing—overaggressive—conceited "superiority complex"—"know-it-all."
3. Inability to express himself clearly — poor voice, diction, grammar.
4. Lack of planning for career — no purpose and goals.
5. Lack of interest and enthusiasm — passive, indifferent.
6. Lack of confidence and poise — nervousness — ill-at-ease.
7. Failure to participate in activities.
8. Overemphasis on money — interest only in best dollar offer.
9. Poor scholastic — just got by.
10. Unwilling to start at the bottom — expects too much.
11. Makes excuses — evasiveness — hedges on unfavorable factors in record.
12. Lack of tact.
13. Lack of maturity.
14. Lack of courtesy — ill-mannered.
15. Condemnation of past employers.
16. Lack of social understanding.
17. Marked dislike for school work.
18. Lack of vitality.
19. Fails to look interviewer in the eye.
20. Limp, fishy handshake.
21. Indecision.
22. Loafs during vacations — lakeside pleasures.
23. Unhappy married life.

24. Friction with parents.
25. Sloppy application blank.
26. Merely shopping around.
27. Wants job only for short time.
28. Little sense of humor.
29. Lack of knowledge of field of specialization.
30. Parents make decisions for him or her.
31. No interest in company or in industry.
32. Emphasis on whom one knows.
33. Unwillingness to go where one is sent.
34. Cynical.
35. Low moral standards.
36. Lazy.
37. Intolerant — strong prejudices.
38. Narrow interests.
39. Spends much time in movies.
40. Poor handling of personal finances.
41. No interest in community activities.
42. Inability to take criticism.
43. Lack of appreciation.
44. Radical ideas.
45. Late to interview without good reason.
46. Never heard of company.
47. Failure to express appreciation for interviewer's time.
48. Asks no questions about the job.
49. High pressure type.
50. Indefinite response to questions.

APPENDIX IV

For the New Year:
A Short Course in Human Relations

The SIX Most Important Words:
"I ADMIT I MADE A MISTAKE"

The FIVE most important words:
"YOU DID A GOOD JOB"

The FOUR most important words:
"WHAT IS YOUR OPINION?"

The THREE most important words:
"IF YOU PLEASE"

The TWO most important words:
"THANK YOU"

The ONE most important word:
"WE"

The LEAST important word:
"I"

APPENDIX V

One key to success is to *Look Like a Winner*. Your bearing, poise, posture, facial expressions, mannerisms, gestures, and the manner in which you wear clothes are ways in which others measure and formulate an opinion of you.

Be physically, mentally, and psychologically alert. Start your day after having had a good night's sleep. Groom yourself carefully. Look yourself over thoroughly in front of a full-length mirror. Check your stance from both a standing and a sitting position before leaving home. Walk briskly with authority when going to the interview; this can convince others that you know what you are doing and where you are going.

Without realizing it, you can often telegraph your emotional state and frame of mind with facial expressions. Think positively, radiantly, and use the power of recall as you think of past victories and successes.

When using expressive gestures, let them reflect purpose and authority when you have something important to divulge to others. Practice these gestures in front of a mirror before actually using them. Do not overexaggerate or underexaggerate — strike a happy medium.

When pursuing your objective *Look Like a Winner*. Walk proudly — reflect confidence, success — it can be yours.

> I am only one, but I am one,
> I can't do everything, but I can do something.
> And what I can do that I ought to do.
> And what I ought to do, by the grace of God, I shall do.
>
> EDWARD HALE
> *former Chaplain, United States Senate*

SELECTED READINGS

BOOKS

1. Amiss, John M. and Sherman, Esther, illustrated by Sheeley, Sidney W. *New Careers in Industry.* New York: McGraw-Hill, Inc. 1946.

2. ARCO Editorial Board. ARCO Course: *Federal Service Entrance Examinations.* New York: Arco Publishing Co. 1965.

3. Bolles, Richard Nelson. *What Color is Your Parachute?* San Francisco, California, 1971 (Author).

4. Boynton, Paul W. *Six Ways to Get a Job.* New York: Harper-Row. 1951.

5. Bovee, Courtland L. *Better Business Writing for Bigger Profits.* Jerico, New York: Exposition Press, Inc. 1970.

6. Collings, Kent J., Lt. Col. *The Second Time Around — Finding a Civilian Career in Mid-life.* Cranston, R.I.: The Carroll Press, 1971.

7. Edlund, M. G. and Edlund, S. W. *Pick Your Job — And Land It!* New York: Prentice-Hall, Inc. 1938.

8. File, Norman and Howroyed, Bernard. *How to Beat the Establishment and Get That Job!* Los Angeles: Apple/One Publishing Co. 1971.

9. Flippo, Edwin B. *Principles of Personnel Management.* New York: McGraw-Hill. 1961.

10. Gates, James E. and Miller, Harold. *Personnel Adjustment to Business.* Englewood Cliffs, New Jersey: Prentice-Hall, Inc. 1958.

11. Gruber, Edward C., ed. *Resumes That Get Jobs.* New York: Arco Publishing Co. 1971.

12. Kingery, Robert Ernest. *How-to-Do-It-Books: A Selected Guide.* New York: Bowker. 1950.

13. Lanham, Elizabeth. *Job Evaluation.* New York: McGraw-Hill. 1955.

14. Lytle, Charles Walter. *Job Evaluation Methods.* New York: Ronald Press Co. 1954.

Selected Readings

15. Morgan, John Smith. *Managing Young Adults.* New York: American Management Association. 1967.
16. New York Life. *Career Opportunities.* Career Information Service, New York Life Ins. Co., New York. 1966.
17. Peterson, Clarence E. *Careers for College Graduates.* New York: Barnes & Noble, Inc. 1969.
18. Schoderbek, Peter P. *Job Enlargement: Key to Performance.* Ann Arbor: Bureau of Industrial Relations, University of Michigan. 1969.
19. Stieri, Emanuele. *The Book of Indoor Hobbies.* New York: McGraw-Hill. 1939.
20. Stone, Charles A. *Frame Your Own Pictures.* Flagstaff, Arizona, 1971 (Author).
21. Thornton, James W., Jr. *The Community College.* New York: John Wiley & Sons, Inc. 1966.
22. Yates, Raymond Francis. *Early American Crafts and Hobbies.* New York: W. Funk. 1954.

JOURNALS

1. Bishop, Joan Fiss. "College Women as Part-Time Workers." *Journal of College Placement,* Dec. 1968–Jan. 1969. (pp. 113–16).
2. Burden, Charles A. "Hiring a Mental Rehabilitant," *Personnel Journal,* Dec. 1971. (pp. 920–23).
3. Butler, William. "The Employer-Student Gap and How to Close It." *Journal of College Placement.* Oct.-Nov. 1968. (pp. 86–90).
4. Fleuter, Douglas L. "Cost Cutting Personnel Practices," *Personnel Journal.* Nov. 1971. (pp. 838–40).
5. Hakel, Milton D. and Mannel, Charles H. "If at First You Don't Succeed." *Journal of College Placement.* Dec. 1968–Jan. 1969. (pp. 65–70).
6. Hakel, Milton D. and Mannel, Charles H. "The Eye of the Beholder." *Journal of College Placement.* Oct.-Nov. 1968. (pp. 39–42).
7. Halloway, Bernard. "Placement Profile — America and Great Britain." *Journal of College Placement.* Apr.-May 1969. (pp. 58–70).
8. Hartman, Richard I. and Gibson, John J. "The Persistent Problem of Employee Absenteeism." *Personnel Journal.* July 1971. (pp. 535–39).
9. Hauck, Robb J. and Stewart, Maude A. "College Men and the Draft: 1969." *The Journal of College Student Personnel.* Nov. 1970. pp. (439–44).
10. Houghton, Cholm G. "The Effective Resume: First Key to Career Success." *Journal of College Placement.* Dec. 1970–Jan. 1971. (pp. 97–100).

11. Hull, Frank W., IV. "The Black Student in Higher Education: A Bibliography." *The Journal of College Student Personnel*. Nov. 1970. (pp. 423–25).

12. Karras, E. J. and McMillan, Ray F., Jr. and Williamson, Thomas R. "Interviewing for a Cultural Match." *Personnel Journal*. Apr. 1971. (pp. 276–79).

13. Katz, I. and Cohen, J. "The Effects of Training Negroes Upon Cooperative Problem Solving in Biracial Teams." *Journal of Abnormal and Social Psychology*. May 1962. (pp. 319–25).

14. Kidd, M. C. "The need for perceptive recruiters." *Journal of College Placement*. Feb.–Mar. 1971. (pp. 89–90).

15. Letchworth, George E. "Women Who Return to College: An Identity-Integrity Approach." *The Journal of College Student Personnel*. Mar. 1970. (pp. 103–06).

16. Luthans, Fred and Hodgetts, Richard M. "How Do Recuriters View Military Experience?" *Personnel Journal*. July 1971. (pp. 530–34).

17. Parrish, John B. "College Women and Jobs: Another look at the 1970's." *Journal of College Placement*. Apr.–May 1971. (pp. 34–40).

18. Pruitt, Anne S. "Black Poor at White Colleges — Personal Growth Goals." *The Journal of College Student Personnel*. Jan. 1970. (pp. 3–7).

19. Robb, Felix, C. "The Three P's: Preparation, Placement, & Performance." *Journal of College Placement*. Feb.–Mar. 1971. (pp. 28–34).

20. Roper, Burns W. "Surveying the World of the Young." *Journal of College Placement*. Oct.–Nov. 1970. (pp. 92–100).

21. Shaw, Arthur C. "College Recruiting: Where will it go in the next decade?" *Journal of College Placement*. Apr.–May 1971. (pp. 55–62).

22. Sherlock, John F. "The Placement Director's Crucial First Year." *Journal of College Placement*. Oct.–Nov. 1970. (pp. 73–80).

23. Shuster, Louis J. "Student Views of Business — A Summation and a Prescription." *Journal of College Placement*. Oct.–Nov. 1968. (pp. 92–100).

24. Soltys, Michael P. "Video-Taped Role Playing." *Journal of College Placement*. Feb.–Mar. 1971. (pp. 55–58).

25. Teach, Leon, "Pre-Selecting the Best Man for a Job." *Personnel Journal*. Oct. 1971. (pp. 796–801).

26. Tyrrell, Richard C. "Campus Recruiting 1985." *Journal of College Placement*. Apr.–May 1971. (pp. 89–93).

27. Varney, Glenn H. and Glass, Elwood G., Jr. "Professionalizing The Campus Interview." *Journal of College Placement*. Feb.–Mar. 1969. (pp. 88–94).

28. Wernimont, Paul F. "What Supervisors and Subordinates Expect of Each Other." *Personnel Journal*. Mar. 1971. (pp. 204–08).

Selected Readings

MAGAZINES

1. *Ebony.* "Black Grad's Problem: Which Job To Take?" May 1969. (pp. 132–34).
2. *Hobbies.* Vol. 77. No. 6. Aug. 1972.
3. *House Beautiful.* "Use and abuse of leisure." Aug. 1969. (pp. 48–49).
4. *Look.* "9 Big Do's and Don'ts For The 1971 Job Hunter." May 18, 1971. (pp. 21–23).
5. *The Retired Officer.* "You May Need SCORE . . . SCORE May Need You." June 1971. (pp. 36–38).
6. *The Retired Officer.* "Employment Clearing House Automates." May 1971. (pp. 38–40).
7. *The Retired Officer.* "Jacqueline Cochran: 'A Renaissance Woman for the 20th Century.'" Sept. 1971. (pp. 28–31).
8. *Time.* "Graduates and Jobs: A Grave New World." May 24, 1971. (pp. 49–59).
9. *U.S. News & World Report.* "Choosing Careers: The Big Shift." May 31, 1971. (pp. 22–24).
10. *U.S. News & World Report.* "Dim Outlook For Summer Jobs." May 24, 1971. (pp. 13–19).
11. *U.S. News & World Report.* "Trends in Labor — Woman's Hours." June 21, 1971. (p. 88).
12. *U.S. News & World Report.* "171 Grads Find A Hard World Waiting." June 26, 1971. (pp. 19–20).
13. *U.S. News & World Report.* "Caring For Others Creates The Spirit of a Nation." Aug. 2, 1971. (pp. 54–57).
14. *U.S. News & World Report.* "Trends in Labor — Pantsuit Decision." Aug. 16, 1971. (p. 70).
15. *U.S. News & World Report.* "Why Women Work." Aug. 23, 1971. (p. 66).
16. *U.S. News & World Report.* "Jobs For College Graduates." Dec. 27, 1971. (pp. 30–33).

PAMPHLETS

Armed Forces Information Service, Department of Defense
"Once A VETERAN — Benefits/Rights/Obligations." Feb. 1965
"Your Personal Affairs." Dec. 6, 1965

Office of the Assistant Secretary of Defense (M&RA)
"College Participation in Specialized Programs for Men Leaving Military Service"

United States Civil Service Commission, Washington, D.C. 20415

"Accent on Youth." BRE-19. June 1969

"Announcing Employment Opportunties For — Clerk, Stenographer, Typist." Announcement No. RP-0-15. Sept. 1970

"Civil Service And The Nation's Progress." Pamphlet 66. Jan. 1969

"expanding opportunities . . . Women in the Federal Government." 1970

"Federal Career Guide for College Students," Denver Civil Service Region. 1970–71

"Federal Employees Facts—POLITICAL ACTIVITY." Federal Employee Facts, No. 2. Mar. 1964

"Federal Jobs Overseas." BRE-18. July 1970

"federal service entrance examination." Sept. 1972

"How To Make The Most of The Merit System." Per. Mgt. Series No. 19. 1968

"Junior Federal Assistant." Announcement No. 411. Nov. 1969

"Matching Person To Job." PS 14. June 1968

"Mid-Level Positions." Announcement No. 413. Jan. 1971

"Retired Military Personnel in Federal Jobs." Per. Mgt. Series No. 21. July 1969

"Senior Level Positions." Announcement No. 408, Rev. Apr. 1971

"Technical Assistant." Announcement No. 409. Sept. 1969

"The Big Pond — Federal Jobs for Engineers, Physical Scientists, Mathematicians." July 1969

"The Human Equation." Pamphlet 76. May 1970

"Upward Mobility For Lower Level Employees." 1970

"Vietnam era Veterans." BRE-28. Oct. 1970

"Working For The USA." Pamphlet 4. Aug. 1970

"Your First Job . . . A Key To Your Future." Pamphlet BRE-10. May 1969

"Your RETIREMENT System." Pamphlet 18, Mar. 1971

United States Department of Labor, Washington, D.C. 20210

"Jobfinding Techniques For Mature Women." Pamphlet 11. Feb. 1970

"Laws on Sex Discrimination in Employment." 1970

"The Law against AGE DISCRIMINATION IN EMPLOYMENT." Sept. 1970

Veterans Administration Information Service

"Federal Benefits for Veterans and Dependents." Jan. 1966

Arizona State Employment Service

"how to . . . PREPARE YOURSELF FOR JOB INTERVIEWS"

"Job Opportunities in Arizona State Service"

Selected Readings

"Merchandising Your Talents"
"Your Job With the State of Arizona"

Check with the State Employment Service in your state for state employment opportunities.